Mark Twain's
Book for
Bad Boys and Girls

Be good + you will be lonesome.

Mark Twain

Mark Twain's
Book for
Bad Boys and Girls

Edited by R. Kent Rasmussen

CONTEMPORARY BOOKS
A TRIBUNE NEW MEDIA/EDUCATION COMPANY

Library of Congress Cataloging-in-Publication Data

Twain, Mark, 1835–1910.
    Mark Twain's book for bad boys and girls / edited by R. Kent
    Rasmussen.
        p.   cm.
    ISBN 0-8092-3398-3 (cloth)
    1. Twain, Mark, 1835–1910—Quotations.   2. Conduct of life—
Quotations, maxims, etc.   3. Quotations, American.
I. Rasmussen, R. Kent.   II. Title.
PS1303.R37   1995
818'.409—dc20   95-32766
                                                              CIP

Copyright © 1995 by R. Kent Rasmussen
All rights reserved
Published by Contemporary Books, Inc.
Two Prudential Plaza, Chicago, Illinois 60601-6790
Manufactured in the United States of America
International Standard Book Number: 0-8092-3398-3
10   9

*F*or Erin, Christopher, Noelle, Heather, and Erik—
who aren't so bad as they like to think.

Contents

Introduction

The nineteenth century produced only a handful of American writers who are still read today—and of these, precious few are read outside of classrooms. Mark Twain is an outstanding exception. Indeed, he may well be the only nineteenth-century American writer as popular today as he was in his own time. He is funny, of course—often hysterically so—but the same thing might be said of dozens of other nineteenth-century humorists whose popularity once rivaled his. The fact that Mark Twain is still widely read while so many others are forgotten suggests that something beyond mere humor makes him special.

The key, I believe, lies in Mark Twain's insights into human nature, his disdain for humbug, and his fundamental honesty. By this, I do not mean that he lied, invented, or exaggerated any less than other writers of his time. Wild exaggeration and distortion, after all, have long been standard techniques of humorous writers. What sets Mark Twain's humor apart is the fact that no matter how outrageous his stories appear to be, some fundamental and important truth usually shines through. Even when his characters behave strangely, there is usually something natural and believable about them. Well understanding the varieties of human nature and motivation, Mark Twain always wrote about real people; he gave them real language to speak and real challenges to overcome. Characters such as his never grow stale.

Although Mark Twain wrote primarily for adults, children have always had a special affection for his work. First, because they find it funny, but more important because it is free of the preachy moralism and falseness that too often spoils children's books. Children delight in reading Mark Twain because he expresses the kinds of truths that they rarely hear elsewhere. He validates many of their most subversive thoughts, reassuring them that they are normal to think that being good is wearing and that being bad is usually a lot more fun. An even more subversive idea runs through much of his writing: namely, that it might be more fun to go to hell than to heaven— doubtless a comforting thought to those (like Huck Finn) who figure they have little chance of reaching the "good place."

In Mark Twain's books—as in real life—bad things happen to good people, just as good things often inexplicably happen to bad people. This latter notion especially appeals to all those children who are constantly hearing from parents and teachers how "bad" they are. Most children, of course, have far more good in them than bad, but that fact should not spoil your pleasure in reading this little volume. Mark Twain, after all, was a pretty good fellow, despite the terrible things that he said about himself.

Kent Rasmussen

A Note on Texts

The selections in this little book derive from a broad range of Mark Twain's writings: from complete sketches and stories to excerpts from novels, travel books, and speeches. Many selections are extracted from longer works. In the latter, deletions are indicated by ellipses; otherwise, nothing has been revised or condensed. Mark Twain's own titles are retained for selections that are complete; titles of extracted material are mostly new. A brief note at the end of each passage indicates its original source.

The extracts from Mark Twain's autobiography merit additional remarks. Mark Twain compiled nearly a half million words of autobiographical material. In 1906–1907, he published about a fifth of this as "Chapters from My Autobiography" in the *North American Review*. His literary executor, Albert Bigelow Paine, later published about 40 percent of the original material (including much that had appeared in the *Review*) as *Mark Twain's Autobiography* in 1924. Sixteen years later, Bernard DeVoto published *Mark Twain in Eruption*, a supplement to Paine's edition that adds another 20 percent of the original material (including some *Review* passages). In 1959, Charles Neider published *The Autobiography of Mark Twain*, a wholly new arrangement with additional material. Finally, Michael J. Kiskis collected the *North American Review* articles in a book titled *Mark Twain's Own Autobiography* in 1990. Although the passages in the present book are taken directly from the three earliest autobiographical publications, many can be found in most of the editions mentioned above.

It is hoped that within a few more years the Mark Twain Project at the University of California will issue the first complete edition of the autobiography. Meanwhile, readers who wish to delve deeper into the nearly bottomless riches of Mark Twain's writings can do no better than to consult the project's definitive editions, which include many works never previously collected in book form.

Mark Twain's
Book for
Bad Boys and Girls

Advice to Young People

*Always do right. This will gratify
some people & astonish the rest.*

*Be respectful to your superiors,
if you have any.*

Advice for Good Little Girls

From early in his writing career, Mark Twain made advice to young people a frequent subject.

Good little girls ought not to make mouths at their teachers for every trifling offense. This retaliation should only be resorted to under peculiarly aggravating circumstances.

If you have nothing but a rag-doll stuffed with saw-dust, while one of your more fortunate little playmates has a costly china one, you should treat her with a show of kindness nevertheless. And you ought not to attempt to make a forcible swap with her unless your conscience would justify you in it, and you know you are able to do it.

You ought never to take your little brother's "chawing-gum" away from him by main force—it is better to rope him in with the promise of the first two dollars and a half you find floating down the river on a grindstone. In the artless simplicity natural to his time of life, he will regard it as a perfectly fair transaction. In all ages of the world this eminently plausible fiction has lured the obtuse infant to financial ruin and disaster.

If at any time you find it necessary to correct your brother, do not correct him with mud—never, on any account, throw mud at him, because it will spoil his clothes. It is better to scald him a little, for then you obtain desirable results—you secure his immediate attention to the lesson you are inculcating, and at the same time your hot water will have a tendency to move impurities from his person—and possibly the skin also, in spots.

If your mother tells you to do a thing, it is wrong to reply that you won't. It is better and more becoming to intimate that you will do as she bids you, and then afterwards act quietly in the matter according to the dictates of your better judgment.

You should ever bear in mind that it is to your kind parents that you are indebted for your food, and your nice bed, and for your beautiful clothes, and for the privilege of staying home from school when you let on that you are sick. Therefore you ought to respect their little prejudices, and humor their little whims and put up with their little foibles, until they get to crowding you too much.

Good little girls always show marked deference for the aged. You ought never to "sass" old people—unless they "sass" you first.

(First published under the same title in
California Youth's Companion, *June 24, 1865)*

Advice for Good Little Boys

You ought never to take anything that don't belong to you—if you can not carry it off.

If you unthinkingly set up a tack in another boy's seat, you ought never to laugh when he sits down on it—unless you can't "hold in."

Good little boys must never tell a lie when the truth will answer just as well. In fact, real good little boys will never tell lies at all—not at all—except in case of the most urgent necessity.

It is wrong to put a sheepskin under your shirt when you know that you are going to get a licking. It is better to retire swiftly to a secret place and weep over your bad conduct until the storm blows over.

You should never do anything wicked and then lay it on your brother, when it is just as convenient to lay it on some other boy.

You ought never to call your aged grandpapa a "rum old file"—except when you want to be unusually funny.

You ought never to knock your little sister down with a club. It is better to use a cat, which is soft. In doing this you must be careful to take the cat by the tail in such a manner that she cannot scratch you.

(First published under the same title in
California Youth's Companion, *June 3, 1865)*

Advice to Youth

In 1882 Mark Twain delivered this address to a teenage girls'
club in Boston.

*B*eing told I would be expected to talk here, I inquired what
sort of a talk I ought to make. They said it should be something suitable to youth—something didactic, instructive, or
something in the nature of good advice. Very well. I have a
few things in my mind which I have often longed to say for
the instruction of the young; for it is in one's tender early years
that such things will best take root and be most enduring and
most valuable.

First, then, I will say to you, my young friends—and I say
it beseechingly, urgingly—

Always obey your parents, when they are present. This is
the best policy in the long run, because if you don't they will
make you. Most parents think they know better than you do,
and you can generally make more by humoring that superstition than you can by acting on your own better judgment.

Be respectful to your superiors, if you have any, also to
strangers, and sometimes to others. If a person offend you,
and you are in doubt as to whether it was intentional or not,
do not resort to extreme measures; simply watch your chance
and hit him with a brick. That will be sufficient. If you shall
find that he had not intended any offense, come out frankly
and confess yourself in the wrong when you struck him;

acknowledge it like a man and say you didn't mean to. Yes, always avoid violence; in this age of charity and kindliness, the time has gone by for such things. Leave dynamite to the low and unrefined.

Go to bed early, get up early—this is wise. Some authorities say get up with the sun; some others say get up with one thing, some with another. But a lark is really the best thing to get up with. It gives you a splendid reputation with everybody to know that you get up with the lark; and if you get the right kind of a lark, and work at him right, you can easily train him to get up at half-past nine, every time—it is no trick at all.

Now as to the matter of lying. You want to be very careful about lying; otherwise you are nearly sure to get caught. Once caught, you can never again be, in the eyes of the good and the pure, what you were before. Many a young person has injured himself permanently through a single clumsy and ill-finished lie, the result of carelessness born of incomplete training. Some authorities hold that the young ought not to lie at all. That, of course, is putting it rather stronger than necessary; still, while I cannot go quite so far as that, I do maintain, and I believe I am right, that the young ought to be temperate in the use of this great art until practice and experience shall give them that confidence, elegance, and precision which alone can make the accomplishment graceful and profitable.

Patience, diligence, painstaking attention to detail—these are the requirements; these, in time, will make the student perfect; upon these, and upon these only, may he rely as the sure foundation for future eminence. Think what tedious years of study, thought, practice, experience, went to the equipment of that peerless old master who was able to impose upon the whole world the lofty and sounding maxim that "truth is mighty and will prevail"—the most majestic compound fracture of fact which any of woman born has yet achieved. For the history of our race, and each individual's experience are sown thick with evidence that a truth is not hard to kill and that a lie told well is immortal.

There in Boston is a monument of the man who discovered anaesthesia; many people are aware, in these latter days, that that man didn't discover it at all, but stole the discovery from another man. Is this truth mighty, and will it prevail? Ah no, my hearers, the monument is made of hardy material, but the lie it tells will outlast it a million years.

An awkward, feeble, leaky lie is a thing which you ought to make it your unceasing study to avoid; such a lie as that has no more real permanence than an average truth. Why, you might as well tell the truth at once and be done with it. A feeble, stupid, preposterous lie will not live two years—except it be a slander upon somebody. It is indestructible, then, of course, but that is no merit of yours. A final word: begin your practice of this gracious and beautiful art early—begin now. If I had begun earlier, I could have learned how.

Never handle firearms carelessly. The sorrow and suffering that have been caused through the innocent but heedless handling of firearms by the young! Only four days ago, right in the next farmhouse to the one where I am spending the summer, a grandmother, old and gray and sweet, one of the loveliest spirits in the land, was sitting at her work, when her young grandson crept in and got down an old, battered, rusty gun which had not been touched for many years and was supposed not to be loaded, and pointed it at her, laughing and threatening to shoot. In her fright she ran screaming and pleading toward the door on the other side of the room; but as she passed him he placed the gun almost against her very breast and pulled the trigger! He had supposed it was not loaded. And he was right—it wasn't. So there wasn't any harm done. It is the only case of that kind I ever heard of.

Therefore, just the same, don't you meddle with old unloaded firearms; they are the most deadly and unerring things that have ever been created by man. You don't have to take any pains at all with them; you don't have to have a rest, you don't have to have any sights on the gun, you don't have to take aim, even. No, you just pick out a relative and bang away, and you are sure to get him. A youth who can't hit a cathedral at thirty yards with a Gatling gun in three-quarters of an hour, can take up an old empty musket and bag his grandmother every time, at a hundred. Think what Waterloo would have been if one of the armies had been boys armed with old muskets supposed not to be loaded, and the other army had been composed of their female relations. The very thought of it makes one shudder.

There are many sorts of books; but good ones are the sort for the young to read. Remember that. They are a great, an inestimable, an unspeakable means of improvement. Therefore be careful in your selections, my young friends; be very careful; confine yourselves exclusively to Robertson's Sermons, Baxter's *Saint's Rest*, *The Innocents Abroad*, and works of that kind.

But I have said enough. I hope you will treasure up the instructions which I have given you, and make them a guide to your feet and a light to your understanding. Build your character thoughtfully and painstakingly upon these precepts, and by and by, when you have got it built, you will be surprised and gratified to see how nicely and sharply it resembles everybody else's.

(speech to the Saturday Morning Club, April 15, 1882)

More than twenty-five years later, Mark Twain added to this advice in a brief speech to a Maryland girls' school. It was the last public speech he ever delivered.

I don't know what to tell you girls to do. Mr. Martin has told you everything you ought to do, and now I must give you some don'ts. There are three things which come to my mind which I consider excellent advice:

First, girls, don't smoke—that is, don't smoke to excess. I am seventy-three and a half years old, and have been smoking seventy-three of them. But I never smoke to excess—that is, I smoke in moderation, only one cigar at a time.

Second, don't drink—that is, don't drink to excess.

Third, don't marry—I mean, to excess.

Honesty is the best policy. That is an old proverb; but you don't want ever to forget it in your journey through life.

(speech at St. Timothy's School, June 9, 1909)

Risky Business

A sin takes on new and real terrors when there seems a chance that it is going to be found out.

What Happens to Boys Who Play Hooky

While writing about a hideous statue that he saw in Italy,
Mark Twain recalled a frightening moment from his youth.

*I*t is hard to forget repulsive things. I remember yet how I
ran off from school once, when I was a boy, and then, pretty
late at night, concluded to climb into the window of my
father's office and sleep on a lounge, because I had a delicacy
about going home and getting thrashed. As I lay on the lounge
and my eyes grew accustomed to the darkness, I fancied I
could see a long, dusky, shapeless thing stretched upon the
floor. A cold shiver went through me. I turned my face to the
wall. That did not answer. I was afraid that that thing would
creep over and seize me in the dark. I turned back and stared
at it for minutes and minutes—they seemed hours. It appeared
to me that the lagging moonlight never, never would get to it.
I turned to the wall and counted twenty, to pass the feverish
time away. I looked—the pale square was nearer. I turned
again and counted fifty—it was almost touching it. With desperate will I turned again and counted one hundred, and
faced about, all in a tremble. A white human hand lay in the
moonlight! Such an awful sinking at the heart—such a sudden gasp for breath! I felt—I can not tell what I felt. When I
recovered strength enough, I faced the wall again. But no boy
could have remained so, with that mysterious hand behind
him. I counted again, and looked—the most of a naked arm
was exposed. I put my hands over my eyes and counted till

I could stand it no longer, and then—the pallid face of a man was there, with the corners of the mouth drawn down, and the eyes fixed and glassy in death! I raised to a sitting posture and glowered on that corpse till the light crept down the bare breast—line by line—inch by inch—past the nipple—and then it disclosed a ghastly stab!

I went away from there. I do not say that I went away in any sort of a hurry, but I simply went—that is sufficient. I went out at the window, and I carried the sash along with me. I did not need the sash, but it was handier to take it than it was to leave it, and so I took it.—I was not scared, but I was considerably agitated.

When I reached home, they whipped me, but I enjoyed it. It seemed perfectly delightful. That man had been stabbed near the office that afternoon, and they carried him in there to doctor him, but he only lived an hour. I have slept in the same room with him often, since then—in my dreams. . . .

(from The Innocents Abroad, *1869, chapter 18)*

Experimenting with the Laws of Gravity

Writing about his 1867 visit to Egypt moved Mark Twain to compare the ancient pyramids to a Missouri hill near the home in which he grew up.

The first time I ever went down the Mississippi, I thought the highest bluff on the river between St. Louis and New Orleans—it was near Selma, Missouri—was probably the highest mountain in the world. It is four hundred and thirteen feet high. It still looms in my memory with undiminished grandeur. I can still see the trees and bushes growing smaller and smaller as I followed them up its huge slant with my eye, till they became a feathery fringe on the distant summit. This symmetrical Pyramid of Cheops—this solid mountain of stone reared by the patient hands of men—this mighty tomb of a forgotten monarch—dwarfs my cherished mountain. For it is four hundred and eighty feet high. In still earlier years than those I have been recalling, Holliday's Hill, in our town, was to me the noblest work of God. It appeared to pierce the skies. It was nearly three hundred feet high. In those days I pondered the subject much, but I never could understand why it did not swathe its summit with never-failing clouds, and crown its majestic brow with everlasting snows. I had heard that such was the custom of great mountains in other parts of the world. I remembered how I worked with another boy, at odd afternoons stolen from study and paid for with stripes, to undermine and start from its bed an immense boulder that rested upon the edge of that hill-top; I remembered how, one Saturday afternoon, we gave three hours of honest effort to the task, and saw at last that our reward was at hand; I remembered how we sat down, then, and wiped the perspiration away, and waited to let a picnic party get out of the way in the road below—and then we started the boulder. It was splendid. It went crashing down the hill-side, tearing up saplings, mowing bushes down like grass, ripping and crushing and smashing every thing in its path—eternally splintered and scattered a wood pile at the foot of the hill, and then sprang from the high bank clear over a dray in the road—the negro glanced up once and dodged—and the next second it made infinitesimal mince-meat of a frame cooper-shop, and the coopers swarmed out like bees. Then we said it was perfectly magnificent, and left. Because the coopers were starting up the hill to inquire. . . .

(from The Innocents Abroad, *1869, chapter 58)*

Not Wasting a Watermelon

*When Mark Twain was a boy, he worked in a newspaper
office in Hannibal, Missouri. Residents of the town still point
to the window where the incident described below took place.*

*I*t was during my first year's apprenticeship in the *Courier*
office that I did a thing which I have been trying to regret for
fifty-five years. It was a summer afternoon and just the kind
of weather that a boy prizes for river excursions and other frol-
ics, but I was a prisoner. The others were all gone holiday-
ing. I was alone and sad. I had committed a crime of some
sort and this was the punishment. I must lose my holiday, and
spend the afternoon in solitude besides. I had the printing-
office all to myself, there in the third story. I had one comfort, and it was a generous one while it lasted. It was the half
of a long and broad watermelon, fresh and red and ripe. I
gouged it out with a knife, and I found accommodation for
the whole of it in my person—though it did crowd me until
the juice ran out of my ears. There remained then the shell,
the hollow shell. It was big enough to do duty as a cradle. I
didn't want to waste it, and I couldn't think of anything to do
with it which could afford entertainment. I was sitting at the
open window which looked out upon the sidewalk of the
main street three stories below, when it occurred to me to drop
it on somebody's head. I doubted the judiciousness of this,
and I had some compunctions about it, too, because so much

of the resulting entertainment would fall to my share and so little to the other person. But I thought I would chance it. I watched out of the window for the right person to come along—the safe person—but he didn't come. Every time there was a candidate he or she turned out to be an unsafe one, and I had to restrain myself. But at last I saw the right one coming. It was my brother Henry. He was the best boy in the whole region. He never did harm to anybody, he never offended anybody. He was exasperatingly good. He had an overflowing abundance of goodness—but not enough to save him this time. I watched his approach with eager interest. He came strolling along, dreaming his pleasant summer dream and not doubting but that Providence had him in His care. If he had known where I was he would have had less confidence in that superstition. As he approached his form became more and more foreshortened. When he was almost under me he was so foreshortened that nothing of him was visible from my high place except the end of his nose and his alternately approaching feet. Then I poised the watermelon, calculated my distance, and let it go, hollow side down. The accuracy of that gunnery was beyond admiration. He had about six steps to make when I let that canoe go, and it was lovely to see those two bodies gradually closing in on each other. If he had had seven steps to make, or five steps to make, my gunnery would have been a failure. But he had exactly the right number to make, and that shell smashed down right on the top of his head and drove him into the earth up to the chin, the chunks of that broken melon flying in every direction like a spray. I wanted to go down there and condole with him, but it would not have been safe. He would have suspected me at once. I expected him to suspect me, anyway, but as he said nothing about this adventure for two or three days—I was watching him in the meantime in order to keep out of danger—I was deceived into believing that this time he didn't suspect me. It was a mistake. He was only waiting for a sure opportunity. Then he landed a cobblestone on the side of my head which raised a bump there so large that I had to wear two hats for a time. I carried this crime to my mother, for I was always anxious to get Henry into trouble with her and could never succeed. I thought that I had a sure case this time when she should come to see that murderous bump. I showed it to her, but she said it was no matter. She didn't need to inquire into the circumstances. She knew I had deserved it, and the best way would be for me to accept it as a valuable lesson, and thereby get profit out of it.

(from his autobiography)

Jim Wolf and the Wasps

Mark Twain's brother Henry was not the only boy on whom he played tricks during his youth. He also enjoyed tormenting a simple-hearted country boy named Jim Wolf who lived with the Clemens family.

*O*ne afternoon I found the upper part of the window in Jim's bedroom thickly cushioned with wasps. Jim always slept on the side of his bed that was against the window. I had what seemed to me a happy inspiration: I turned back the bed-clothes and, at cost of one or two stings, brushed the wasps down and collected a few hundred of them on the sheet on that side of the bed, then turned the covers over them and made prisoners of them. I made a deep crease down the center of the bed to protect the front side from invasion by them, and then at night I offered to sleep with Jim. He was willing.

I made it a point to be in bed first to see if my side of it was still a safe place to rest in. It was. None of the wasps had passed the frontier. As soon as Jim was ready for bed I blew out the candle and let him climb in in the dark. He was talk-ing as usual but I couldn't answer, because by anticipation I was suffocating with laughter, and although I gagged myself with a hatful of the sheet I was on the point of exploding all the time. Jim stretched himself out comfortably, still pleasantly chatting; then his talk began to break and become disjointed; separations intervened between his words and each separation was emphasized by a more or less sudden and violent twitch of his body, and I knew that the immigrants were getting in their work. I knew I ought to evince some sympathy, and ask what was the matter, but I couldn't do it because I should laugh if I tried. Presently he stopped talking altogether—that is on the subject which he had been pursuing, and he said, "There is something in this bed."

I knew it but held my peace.

He said, "There's thousands of them."

Then he said he was going to find out what it was. He reached down and began to explore. The wasps resented this intrusion and began to stab him all over and everywhere. Then he said he had captured one of them and asked me to strike a light. I did it, and when he climbed out of bed his shirt was black with half-crushed wasps dangling by one hind leg, and in his two hands he held a dozen prisoners that were stinging and stabbing him with energy, but his grit was good and he held them fast. By the light of the candle he identified them, and said, "Wasps!"

It was his last remark for the night. He added nothing to it. In silence he uncovered his side of the bed and, dozen by dozen, he removed the wasps to the floor and beat them to a pulp with the bootjack, with earnest and vindictive satisfaction, while I shook the bed with mute laughter—laughter which was not all a pleasure to me, for I had the sense that his silence was ominous. The work of extermination being finally completed, he blew out the light and returned to bed and seemed to compose himself to sleep—in fact he did lie stiller than anybody else could have done in the circumstances.

I remained awake as long as I could and did what I could to keep my laughter from shaking the bed and provoking suspicion, but even my fears could not keep me awake forever and I finally fell asleep and presently woke again—under persuasion of circumstances. Jim was kneeling on my breast and pounding me in the face with both fists. It hurt—but he was knocking all the restraints of my laughter loose; I could not contain it any longer and I laughed until all my body was exhausted, and my face, as I believed, battered to a pulp.

Jim never afterward referred to that episode and I had better judgment than to do it myself, for he was a third longer than I was, although not any wider.

I played many practical jokes upon him but they were all cruel and all barren of wit. Any brainless swindler could have invented them. When a person of mature age perpetrates a practical joke it is fair evidence, I think, that he is weak in the head and hasn't enough heart to signify.

(from his autobiography)

Skating Without Permission

Mark Twain remembered just how foolish boys could be while writing his autobiography in 1906. He recalled an incident that occurred around 1849, when he was about fourteen.

Tom Nash was a boy of my own age—the postmaster's son. The Mississippi was frozen across, and he and I went skating one night, probably without permission. I cannot see why we should go skating in the night unless without permission, for there could be no considerable amusement to be gotten out of skating at midnight if nobody was going to object to it. About midnight, when we were more than half a mile out toward the Illinois shore, we heard some ominous rumbling and grinding and crashing going on between us and the home side of the river, and we knew what it meant—the river was breaking up. We started for home, pretty badly scared. We flew along at full speed whenever the moonlight sifting down between the clouds enabled us to tell which was ice and which was water. In the pauses we waited, started again whenever there was a good bridge of ice, paused again when we came to naked water, and waited in distress until a floating vast cake should bridge that place. It took us an hour to make the trip—a trip which we made in a misery of apprehension all the time. But at last we arrived within a very brief distance of the shore. We waited again. There was another place that needed bridging. All about us the ice was plunging and grinding along and piling itself up in mountains on the shore, and the dangers were increasing, not diminishing. We grew very impatient to get to solid ground, so we started too early and went springing from cake to cake. Tom made a miscalculation and fell short. He got a bitter bath, but he was so close to shore that he only had to swim a stroke or two—then his feet struck hard bottom and he crawled out. I arrived a little later, without accident. We had been in a drenching perspiration and Tom's bath was a disaster for him. He took to his bed, sick, and had a procession of diseases. The closing one was scarlet-fever, and he came out of it stone deaf. Within a year or two speech departed, of course. But some years later he was taught to talk, after a fashion—one couldn't always make out what it was he was trying to say. Of course he could not modulate his voice, since he couldn't hear himself talk. When he supposed he was talking low and confidentially, you could hear him in Illinois.

Four years ago (1902) I was invited by the University of Missouri to come out there and receive the honorary degree of LL.D. I took that opportunity to spend a week in Hannibal—a city now, a village in my day. It had been fifty-five years since Tom Nash and I had had that adventure. When I was at the railway station ready to leave Hannibal, there was a great crowd of citizens there. I saw Tom Nash approaching me across a vacant space, and I walked toward him, for I recognized him at once. He was old and white-headed, but the boy of fifteen was still visible in him. He came up to me, made a trumpet of his hands at my ear, nodded his head toward the citizens, and said, confidentially—in a yell like a fog horn—

"Same damned fools, Sam."

(from his autobiography)

Nasty Tricks

During three-fourths of my life I have held the
practical joker in limitless contempt and detestation;
I have despised him as I have despised no other criminal,
and when I am delivering my opinion about him
the reflection that I have been a practical joker myself
seems to increase my bitterness rather than to modify it.

Disordering Auntie's Mind

Many incidents in the Tom Sawyer and Huckleberry Finn stories derive from Mark Twain's own experiences during the idyllic summers that he spent at the farm of his aunt and uncle near Florida, Missouri, when he was a boy.

Along outside of the front fence ran the country road, dusty in the summertime, and a good place for snakes—they liked to lie in it and sun themselves; when they were rattlesnakes or puff adders, we killed them; when they were black snakes, or racers, or belonged to the fabled "hoop" breed, we fled, without shame; when they were "house snakes," or "garters," we carried them home and put them in Aunt Patsy's work basket for a surprise; for she was prejudiced against snakes, and always when she took the basket in her lap and they began to climb out of it, it disordered her mind. She never could seem to get used to them; her opportunities went for nothing. And she was always cold towards bats, too, and could not bear them; and yet I think a bat is as friendly a bird as there is. My mother was Aunt Patsy's sister and had the same wild superstitions. A bat is beautifully soft and silky; I do not know any creature that is pleasanter to the touch or is more grateful for caressings, if offered in the right spirit. I know all about these coleoptera, because our great cave, three miles below Hannibal, was multitudinously stocked with them, and often I brought them home to amuse my mother with. It was easy to manage if it was a school day, because then I had ostensibly been to school and hadn't any bats. She was not a suspicious person, but full of trust and confidence; and when I said, "There's something in my coat pocket for you," she would put her hand in. But she always took it out again, herself; I didn't have to tell her. It was remarkable, the way she couldn't learn to like private bats. The more experience she had, the more she could not change her views. . . .

(from his autobiography)

Jim Wolf and the Cats

Mark Twain learned early that the bashful make particularly good targets for practical jokes. He often retold this story about Jim Wolf's experience with the cats.

*I*t was back in those far-distant days—1848 or '9—that Jim Wolf came to us. He was from a hamlet thirty or forty miles back in the country, and he brought all his native sweetnesses and gentlenesses and simplicities with him. He was approaching seventeen, a grave and slender lad, trustful, honest, honorable, a creature to love and cling to. And he was incredibly bashful.

It is to this kind that untoward things happen. My sister gave a "candy-pull" on a winter's night. I was too young to be of the company, and Jim was too diffident. I was sent up to bed early, and Jim followed of his own motion. His room was in the new part of the house and his window looked out on the roof of the L annex. That roof was six inches deep in snow, and the snow had an ice crust upon it which was as slick as glass. Out of the comb of the roof projected a short chimney, a common resort for sentimental cats on moonlight nights—and this was a moonlight night. Down at the eaves, below the chimney, a canopy of dead vines spread away to some posts, making a cozy shelter, and after an hour or two the rollicking crowd of young ladies and gentlemen grouped themselves in its shade, with their saucers of liquid and piping-hot candy disposed about them on the frozen ground to cool. There was joyous chaffing and joking and laughter— peal upon peal of it.

About this time a couple of old disreputable tom-cats got up on the chimney and started a heated argument about something; also about this time I gave up trying to get to sleep and went visiting to Jim's room. He was awake and fuming about the cats and their intolerable yowling. I asked him, mockingly, why he didn't climb out and drive them away. He was nettled, and said over-boldly that for two cents he *would*.

It was a rash remark and was probably repented of before it was fairly out of his mouth. But it was too late—he was committed. I knew him; and I knew he would rather break his neck than back down, if I egged him on judiciously.

"Oh, of course you would! Who's doubting it?"

It galled him, and he burst out, with sharp irritation— "Maybe *you* doubt it!"

"I? Oh no! I shouldn't think of such a thing. You are always doing wonderful things. With your mouth."

He was in a passion now. He snatched on his yarn socks and began to raise the window, saying in a voice quivering with anger—

"*You* think I dasn't—*you* do! Think what you blame please.—*I* don't care what you think. I'll show you!"

The window made him rage; it wouldn't stay up. I said— "Never mind, I'll hold it."

Indeed, I would have done anything to help. I was only a boy, and was already in a radiant heaven of anticipation. He climbed carefully out, clung to the window-sill until his feet were safely placed, then began to pick his perilous way on all fours along the glassy comb, a foot and a hand on each side of it. I believe I enjoy it now as much as I did then: yet it is nearly fifty years ago. The frosty breeze flapped his short shirt about his lean legs; the crystal roof shone like polished marble in the intense glory of the moon; the unconscious cats sat erect upon the chimney, alertly watching each other, lashing their tails and pouring out their hollow grievances; and slowly and cautiously Jim crept on, flapping as he went, the gay and frolicsome young creatures under the vine-canopy unaware, and outraging these solemnities with their misplaced laughter. Every time Jim slipped I had a hope; but always on he crept and disappointed it. At last he was within reaching distance. He paused, raised himself carefully up, measured his distance deliberately, then made a frantic grab at the nearest cat—and missed. Of course he lost his balance. His heels flew up, he struck on his back, and like a rocket he darted down the roof feet first, crashed through the dead vines, and landed in a sitting posture in fourteen saucers of red-hot candy, in the midst of all that party—and dressed as *he* was—this lad who could not look a girl in the face with his clothes on. There was a wild scramble and a storm of shrieks, and Jim fled up the stairs, dripping broken crockery all the way. . . .

(from his autobiography)

Nicodemus Dodge and the Skeleton

Jim Wolf appears frequently in Mark Twain's writings. In one of his earliest appearances, he is the not-so-innocent "Nicodemus Dodge" in A Tramp Abroad.

When I was a boy in a printing-office in Missouri, a loose-jointed, long-legged, tow-headed, jeans-clad, countrified cub of about sixteen lounged in one day, and without removing his hands from the depths of his trousers pockets or taking off his faded ruin of a slouch hat, whose broken rim hung limp and ragged about his eyes and ears like a bug-eaten cabbage leaf, stared indifferently around, then leaned his hip against the editor's table, crossed his mighty brogans, aimed at a distant fly from a crevice in his upper teeth, laid him low, and said with composure:

"Whar's the boss?" . . .

After Dodge is hired, he takes up residence in a broken-down ghostly shack in a secluded and lonely spot.

The village smarties recognized a treasure in Nicodemus, right away—a butt to play jokes on. It was easy to see that he was inconceivably green and confiding. George Jones had the glory of perpetrating the first joke on him; he gave him a cigar with a firecracker in it and winked to the crowd to come; the thing exploded presently and swept away the bulk of Nicodemus's eyebrows and eyelashes. He simply said:

"I consider them kind of seeg'yars dangersome,"—and seemed to suspect nothing. The next evening Nicodemus waylaid George and poured a bucket of ice-water over him.

One day, while Nicodemus was in swimming, Tom McElroy "tied" his clothes. Nicodemus made a bonfire of Tom's by way of retaliation.

A third joke was played upon Nicodemus a day or two later—he walked up the middle aisle of the village church,

Sunday night, with a staring handbill pinned between his shoulders. The joker spent the remainder of the night, after church, in the cellar of a deserted house, and Nicodemus sat on the cellar door till toward breakfast-time to make sure that the prisoner remembered that if any noise was made, some rough treatment would be the consequence. The cellar had two feet of stagnant water in it, and was bottomed with six inches of soft mud.

But I wander from the point. It was the subject of skeletons that brought this boy back to my recollection. Before a very long time had elapsed, the village smarties began to feel an uncomfortable consciousness of not having made a very shining success out of their attempts on the simpleton from "old Shelby." Experimenters grew scarce and chary. Now the young doctor came to the rescue. There was delight and applause when he proposed to scare Nicodemus to death, and explained how he was going to do it. He had a noble new skeleton—the skeleton of the late and only local celebrity, Jimmy Finn, the village drunkard—a grisly piece of property which he had bought of Jimmy Finn himself, at auction, for fifty dollars, under great competition, when Jimmy lay very sick in the tanyard a fortnight before his death. The fifty dollars had gone promptly for whisky and had considerably hurried up the change of ownership in the skeleton. The doctor would put Jimmy Finn's skeleton in Nicodemus's bed!

This was done—about half past ten in the evening. About Nicodemus's usual bedtime—midnight—the village jokers came creeping stealthily through the jimpson weeds and sun-flowers toward the lonely frame den. They reached the window and peeped in. There sat the long-legged pauper, on his bed, in a very short shirt, and nothing more; he was dangling his legs contentedly back and forth, and wheezing the music of "Camptown Races" out of a paper-overlaid comb which he was pressing against his mouth; by him lay a new jewsharp, a new top, a solid india-rubber ball, a handful of painted marbles, five pounds of "store" candy, and a well-gnawed slab of gingerbread as big and as thick as a volume of sheet-music. He had sold the skeleton to a traveling quack for three dollars and was enjoying the result!

(from A Tramp Abroad, *1880, chapter 23)*

Defying Authority

Always acknowledge a fault frankly. This will throw those in authority off their guard and give you an opportunity to commit more.

Never tell the truth to people who are not worthy of it.

First Day of School

Mark Twain's first day in school taught him one of his first lessons in respecting authority.

*M*y school days began when I was four years and a half old. There were no public schools in Missouri in those early days, but there were two private schools—terms twenty-five cents per week per pupil and collect it if you can. Mrs. Horr taught the children in a small log house at the southern end of Main Street. Mr. Sam Cross taught the young people of larger growth in a frame schoolhouse on the hill. I was sent to Mrs. Horr's school and I remember my first day in that little log house with perfect clearness, after these sixty-five years and upwards—at least I remember an episode of that first day. I broke one of the rules and was warned not to do it again, and was told that the penalty for a second breach was a whipping. I presently broke the rule again and Mrs. Horr told me to go out and find a switch and fetch it. I was glad she appointed me, for I believed that I could select a switch suitable to the occasion with more judiciousness than anybody else.

In the mud I found a cooper's shaving of the old-time pattern, oak, two inches broad, a quarter of an inch thick, and rising in a shallow curve at one end. There were nice new shavings of the same breed close by but I took this one, although it was rotten. I carried it to Mrs. Horr, presented it, and stood before her in an attitude of meekness and resignation which seemed to me calculated to win favor and sympathy, but it did not happen. She divided a long look of strong disapprobation equally between me and the shaving; then she called me by my entire name, Samuel Langhorne Clemens— probably the first time I had ever heard it all strung together in one procession—and said she was ashamed of me. I was to learn later that when a teacher calls a boy by his entire name it means trouble. She said she would try and appoint a boy with a better judgment than mine in the matter of switches, and it saddens me yet to remember how many faces lighted up with the hope of getting that appointment. Jim Dunlap got it, and when he returned with the switch of his choice I recognized that he was an expert.

(from his autobiography)

An Entertainment More Precious
than Fishing and Swimming

*As a teenager, Mark Twain apprenticed in a print shop
alongside Wales McCormick, an older boy who taught him
early lessons in rebellion. On one occasion the founder of the
Campbellite religious sect engaged the shop to print a long
sermon in a sixteen-page pamphlet—a job that threatened to
ruin the boys' Saturday afternoon off.*

We set up the great book in pages—eight pages to a form—
and by help of a printer's manual we managed to get the pages
in their apparently crazy but really sane places on the impos-
ing-stone. We printed that form on a Thursday. Then we set
up the remaining eight pages, locked them into a form, and
struck a proof. Wales read the proof, and presently was aghast,
for he had struck a snag. And it was a bad time to strike a
snag, because it was Saturday; it was approaching noon; Saturday afternoon was our holiday, and we wanted to get away
and go fishing. At such a time as this Wales struck that snag
and showed us what had happened. He had left out a couple
of words in a thin-spaced page of solid matter and there
wasn't another break-line for two or three pages ahead. What
in the world was to be done? Overrun all those pages in order
to get in the two missing words? Apparently there was no
other way. It would take an hour to do it. Then a revise must

be sent to the great minister; we must wait for him to read
the revise; if he encountered any errors we must correct them.
It looked as if we might lose half the afternoon before we
could get away. Then Wales had one of his brilliant ideas. In
the line in which the "out" had been made occurred the name
Jesus Christ. Wales reduced it in the French way to J. C. It
made room for the missing words, but it took 99 per cent of
the solemnity out of a particularly solemn sentence. We sent
off the revise and waited. We were not intending to wait long.
In the circumstances we meant to get out and go fishing before
that revise should get back, but we were not speedy enough.
Presently that great Alexander Campbell appeared at the far
end of that sixty-foot room, and his countenance cast a gloom
over the whole place. He strode down to our end and what
he said was brief, but it was very stern, and it was to the
point. He read Wales a lecture. He said, "So long as you live,
don't you ever diminish the Saviour's name again. Put it *all*
in." He repeated this admonition a couple of times to empha-
size it, then he went away.

In that day the common swearers of the region had a way
of their own of *emphasizing* the Saviour's name when they
were using it profanely, and this fact intruded itself into
Wales's incorrigible mind. It offered him an opportunity
for a momentary entertainment which seemed to him to be
more precious and more valuable than even fishing and swimming could afford. So he imposed upon himself the long and
weary and dreary task of overrunning all those three pages

in order to improve upon his former work and incidentally
and thoughtfully improve upon the great preacher's admonition. He enlarged the offending J. C. into Jesus H. Christ.
Wales knew that that would make a prodigious trouble, and
it did. But it was not in him to resist it. He had to succumb
to the law of his make. I don't remember what his punishment
was, but he was not the person to care for that. He had already
collected his dividend.

(from his autobiography)

Seventeen New Ways to Kill Mr. Brown

*In the late 1850s, Mark Twain spent two years apprenticing
as a "cub" on the Mississippi River before he became a
licensed steamboat pilot. When his mentor, Horace Bixby,
was away from the river he worked with other men, including
a petty tyrant named William Brown, on the steamboat*
Pennsylvania.

*H*e was a middle-aged, long, slim, bony, smooth-shaven,
horse-faced, ignorant, stingy, malicious, snarling, fault-hunt-
ing, mote-magnifying tyrant. I early got the habit of coming
on watch with dread at my heart. No matter how good a time
I might have been having with the off-watch below, and no
matter how high my spirits might be when I started aloft, my
soul became lead in my body the moment I approached the
pilot-house. . . .

*After enumerating Brown's petty cruelties, Mark Twain
recalls his own homicidal fantasies.*

I often wanted to kill Brown, but this would not answer. A
cub had to take everything his boss gave, in the way of vig-
orous comment and criticism; and we all believed that there
was a United States law making it a penitentiary offence to
strike or threaten a pilot who was on duty. However, I could
imagine myself killing Brown; there was no law against that;
and that was the thing I used always to do the moment I was
abed. Instead of going over my river in my mind, as was my
duty, I threw business aside for pleasure, and killed Brown.
I killed Brown every night for months; not in old, stale, com-
monplace ways, but in new and picturesque ones—ways that
were sometimes surprising for freshness of design and ghast-
liness of situation and environment.

Brown was *always* watching for a pretext to find fault; and
if he could find no plausible pretext, he would invent one. He
would scold you for shaving a shore, and for not shaving it;
for hugging a bar, and for not hugging it; for "pulling down"
when not invited, and for *not* pulling down when not invited;
for firing up without orders, and for waiting *for* orders. In a
word, it was his invariable rule to find fault with *everything*
you did; and another invariable rule of his was to throw all
his remarks (to you) into the form of an insult. . . .

After one particularly unpleasant day . . .

When I went to bed that night, I killed Brown in seventeen different ways—all of them new.

Two trips later, I got into serious trouble. Brown was steering; I was "pulling down." My younger brother appeared on the hurricane-deck, and shouted to Brown to stop at some landing or other, a mile or so below. Brown gave no intimation that he had heard anything. But that was his way: he never condescended to take notice of an under-clerk. The wind was blowing; Brown was deaf (although he always pretended he wasn't), and I very much doubted if he had heard the order. If I had had two heads, I would have spoken; but as I had only one, it seemed judicious to take care of it; so I kept still.

Presently, sure enough, we went sailing by that plantation. Captain Klinefelter appeared on the deck, and said:

"Let her come around, sir, let her come around. Didn't Henry tell you to land here?"

"*No*, sir!"

"I sent him up to do it."

"He *did* come up; and that's all the good it done, the dodderned fool. He never said anything."

"Didn't *you* hear him?" asked the captain of me.

Of course I didn't want to be mixed up in this business, but there was no way to avoid it; so I said:

"Yes, sir."

I knew what Brown's next remark would be, before he uttered it. It was:

"Shut your mouth! you never heard anything of the kind."

I closed my mouth, according to instructions. An hour later Henry entered the pilot-house, unaware of what had been going on. He was a thoroughly inoffensive boy, and I was sorry to see him come, for I knew Brown would have no pity on him. Brown began, straightway:

"Here! Why didn't you tell me we'd got to land at that plantation?"

"I did tell you, Mr. Brown."

"It's a lie!"

I said:

"You lie, yourself. He did tell you."

Brown glared at me in unaffected surprise; and for as much as a moment he was entirely speechless; then he shouted to me:

"I'll attend to your case in a half a minute!" then to Henry, "And you leave the pilot-house; out with you!"

It was pilot law, and must be obeyed. The boy started out, and even had his foot on the upper step outside the door, when Brown, with a sudden access of fury, picked up a ten-pound lump of coal and sprang after him; but I was between, with a heavy stool, and I hit Brown a good honest blow which stretched him out.

I had committed the crime of crimes—I had lifted my hand against a pilot on duty! I supposed I was booked for the penitentiary sure, and couldn't be booked any surer if I went on and squared my long account with this person while I had the chance; consequently I stuck to him and pounded him with my fists a considerable time. I do not know how long, the pleasure of it probably made it seem longer than it really was; but in the end he struggled free and jumped up and sprang to the wheel: a very natural solicitude, for, all this time, here was this steamboat tearing down the river at the rate of fifteen miles an hour and nobody at the helm! However, Eagle Bend was two miles wide at this bank-full stage, and correspondingly long and deep: and the boat was steering herself straight down the middle and taking no chances. Still, that was only luck— a body *might* have found her charging into the woods.

Perceiving at a glance that the *Pennsylvania* was in no danger, Brown gathered up the big spy-glass, war-club fashion, and ordered me out of the pilot-house with more than Comanche bluster. But I was not afraid of him now; so, instead of going, I tarried, and criticized his grammar; I reformed his ferocious speeches for him, and put them into good English, calling his attention to the advantage of pure English over the bastard dialect of the Pennsylvanian collieries whence he was extracted. He could have done his part to admiration in a cross-fire of mere vituperation, of course;

but he was not equipped for this species of controversy; so he presently laid aside his glass and took the wheel, muttering and shaking his head; and I retired to the bench. The racket had brought everybody to the hurricane-deck, and I trembled when I saw the old captain looking up from the midst of the crowd. I said to myself, "Now I *am* done for!" For although, as a rule, he was so fatherly and indulgent toward the boat's family, and so patient of minor shortcomings, he could be stern enough when the fault was worth it.

I tried to imagine what he *would* do to a cub pilot who had been guilty of such a crime as mine, committed on a boat guard-deep with costly freight and alive with passengers. Our watch was nearly ended. I thought I would go and hide somewhere till I got a chance to slide ashore. So I slipped out of the pilot-house, and down the steps, and around to the texas-door, and was in the act of gliding within, when the captain confronted me! I dropped my head, and he stood over me in silence a moment or two, then said impressively:

"Follow me."

I dropped into his wake; he led the way to his parlor in the forward end of the texas. We were alone, now. He closed the after door; then moved slowly to the forward one and closed that. He sat down; I stood before him. He looked at me some little time, then said:

"So you have been fighting Mr. Brown?"

I answered meekly:

"Yes, sir."

"Do you know that that is a very serious matter?"

"Yes, sir."

"Are you aware that this boat was ploughing down the river fully five minutes with no one at the wheel?"

"Yes, sir."

"Did you strike him first?"

"Yes, sir."

"What with?"

"A stool, sir."

"Hard?"

"Middling, sir."

"Did it knock him down?"

"He—he fell, sir."

"Did you follow it up? Did you do anything further?"

"Yes, sir."

"What did you do?"

"Pounded him, sir."

"Pounded him?"

"Yes, sir."

"Did you pound him much? that is, severely?"

"One might call it that, sir, maybe."

"I'm deucéd glad of it! Hark ye, never mention that I said that. You have been guilty of a great crime; and don't you ever be guilty of it again, on this boat. *But*—lay for him ashore! Give him a good sound thrashing, do you hear? I'll pay the expenses. Now go—and mind you, not a word of this to anybody. Clear out with you! You've been guilty of a great crime, you whelp!"

I slid out, happy with the sense of a close shave and a mighty deliverance; and I heard him laughing to himself and slapping his fat thighs after I had closed his door.

When Brown came off watch he went straight to the captain, who was talking with some passengers on the boiler-deck, and demanded that I be put ashore in New Orleans—and added:

"I'll never turn a wheel on this boat again while that cub stays."

The captain said:

"But he needn't come round when you are on watch, Mr. Brown."

"I won't even stay on the same boat with him. *One* of us has got to go ashore."

"Very well," said the captain, "let it be yourself," and resumed his talk with the passengers.

During the brief remainder of the trip I knew how an emancipated slave feels; for I was an emancipated slave myself. . . .

(from Life on the Mississippi, *1883, chapters 18–19)*

Taking Care of Business

*Work and play are words used to describe
the same thing under differing conditions.*

*It is better to take what does not belong to you
than to let it lie around neglected.*

Tom Sawyer Slaughters the Innocents

After Tom gets into trouble, his Aunt Polly orders him to spend Saturday whitewashing a fence. A sudden insight into the difference between "work" and "play" gives Tom an idea that not only gets the job done, but makes him a hefty profit.

Saturday morning was come, and all the summer world was bright and fresh, and brimming with life. There was a song in every heart; and if the heart was young the music issued at the lips. There was cheer in every face and a spring in every step. The locust trees were in bloom and the fragrance of the blossoms filled the air. Cardiff Hill, beyond the village and above it, was green with vegetation, and it lay just far enough away to seem a Delectable Land, dreamy, reposeful and inviting.

Tom appeared on the sidewalk with a bucket of whitewash and a long-handled brush. He surveyed the fence, and all gladness left him and a deep melancholy settled down upon his spirit. Thirty yards of board fence, nine feet high. Life to him seemed hollow, and existence but a burden. Sighing, he dipped his brush and passed it along the topmost plank; repeated the operation; did it again; compared the insignificant whitewashed streak with the far-reaching continent of unwhitewashed fence, and sat down on a tree-box discouraged. Jim came skipping out at the gate with a tin pail, and singing "Buffalo Gals." Bringing water from the town pump

had always been hateful work in Tom's eyes, before, but now
it did not strike him so. He remembered that there was company at the pump. White, mulatto and negro boys and girls
were always there waiting their turns, resting, trading playthings, quarreling, fighting, skylarking. And he remembered
that although the pump was only a hundred and fifty yards
off, Jim never got back with a bucket of water under an hour—
and even then somebody generally had to go after him. Tom
said:

"Say, Jim, I'll fetch the water if you'll whitewash some."

Jim shook his head and said:

"Can't, Mars Tom. Ole missis, she tole me I got to go an'
git dis water an' not stop foolin' roun' wid anybody. She say
she spec' Mars Tom gwyne to ax me to whitewash, an' so she
tole me go 'long an' 'tend to my own business—she 'lowed
she'd 'tend to de whitewashin'."

"Oh, never you mind what she said, Jim. That's the way
she always talks. Gimme the bucket—I won't be gone only a
minute. *She* won't ever know."

"Oh, I dasn't, Mars Tom. Ole missis she'd take an' tar de
head off'n me. 'Deed she would."

"*She!* She never licks anybody—whacks 'em over the head
with her thimble—and who cares for that, I'd like to know.
She talks awful, but talk don't hurt—anyways it don't if she
don't cry. Jim, I'll give you a marvel. I'll give you a white
alley!"

Jim began to waver.

"White alley, Jim! And it's a bully taw."

"My! Dat's a mighty gay marvel, *I* tell you! But Mars Tom I's powerful 'fraid ole missis—"

"And besides, if you will, I'll show you my sore toe."

Jim was only human—this attraction was too much for him. He put down his pail, took the white alley, and bent over the toe with absorbing interest while the bandage was being unwound. In another moment he was flying down the street with his pail and a tingling rear, Tom was whitewashing with vigor, and aunt Polly was retiring from the field with a slipper in her hand and triumph in her eye.

But Tom's energy did not last. He began to think of the fun he had planned for this day, and his sorrows multiplied. Soon the free boys would come tripping along on all sorts of delicious expeditions, and they would make a world of fun of him for having to work—the very thought of it burnt him like fire. He got out his worldly wealth and examined it—bits of toys, marbles and trash; enough to buy an exchange of *work*, maybe, but not half enough to buy so much as half an hour of pure freedom. So he returned his straightened means to his pocket and gave up the idea of trying to buy the boys. At this dark and hopeless moment an inspiration burst upon him! Nothing less than a great, magnificent inspiration!

He took up his brush and went tranquilly to work. Ben Rogers hove in sight presently—the very boy, of all boys, whose ridicule he had been dreading. Ben's gait was the hop-skip-and-jump—proof enough that his heart was light and his anticipations high. He was eating an apple, and giving a long, melodious whoop, at intervals, followed by a deep-toned ding-dong-dong, ding-dong-dong, for he was personating a steamboat. As he drew near, he slackened speed, took the middle of the street, leaned far over to starboard and rounded to ponderously and with laborious pomp and circumstance— for he was personating the "Big Missouri," and considered himself to be drawing nine feet of water. He was boat and captain and engine-bells combined, so he had to imagine himself standing on his own hurricane deck giving the orders and executing them:

"Stop her, sir! Ting-a-ling-ling!" The headway ran almost out and he drew up slowly toward the side-walk.

"Ship up to back! Ting-a-ling-ling!" His arms straightened and stiffened down his sides.

"Set her back on the stabboard! Ting-a-ling-ling! Chow! ch-chow-wow! Chow!" His right hand, meantime, describing stately circles—for it was representing a forty-foot wheel.

"Let her go back on the labbord! Ting-a-ling-ling! Chow-ch-chow-chow!" The left hand began to describe circles.

"Stop the stabboard! Ting-a-ling-ling! Stop the labbord! Come ahead on the stabboard! Stop her! Let your outside turn over slow! Ting-a-ling-ling! Chow-ow-ow! Get out that head-line! *Lively*, now! Come—out with your spring-line— what're you about there! Take a turn round that stump with the bight of it! Stand by that stage, now—let her go! Done with the engines, sir! Ting-a-ling-ling! *Sh't! s'sh't! sh't!*" (trying the gauge-cocks.)

Tom went on whitewashing—paid no attention to the steamboat. Ben stared a moment and then said:

"Hi-*yi*! *You're* up a stump, ain't you!"

No answer. Tom surveyed his last touch with the eye of an artist; then he gave his brush another gentle sweep and surveyed the result, as before. Ben ranged up alongside of him. Tom's mouth watered for the apple, but he stuck to his work. Ben said:

"Hello, old chap, you got to work, hey?"

Tom wheeled suddenly and said:

"Why it's you, Ben! I warn't noticing."

"Say—*I*'m going in a-swimming, *I* am. Don't you wish you could? But of course you'd druther *work*—wouldn't you? 'Course you would!"

Tom contemplated the boy a bit, and said:

"What do you call work?"

"Why, ain't *that* work?"

Tom resumed his whitewashing, and answered carelessly:

"Well, maybe it is, and maybe it ain't. All I know, is, it suits Tom Sawyer."

"Oh come, now, you don't mean to let on that you *like* it?"

The brush continued to move.

"Like it? Well I don't see why I oughtn't to like it. Does a boy get a chance to whitewash a fence every day?"

That put the thing in a new light. Ben stopped nibbling his apple. Tom swept his brush daintily back and forth—stepped back to note the effect—added a touch here and there—criticised the effect again—Ben watching every move and getting more and more interested, more and more absorbed. Presently he said:

"Say, Tom, let *me* whitewash a little."

Tom considered; was about to consent; but he altered his mind:

"No—no—I reckon it wouldn't hardly do, Ben. You see, aunt Polly's awful particular about this fence—right here on the street, you know—but if it was the back fence I wouldn't mind and *she* wouldn't. Yes, she's awful particular about this fence; it's got to be done very careful; I reckon there ain't one boy in a thousand, maybe two thousand, that can do it the way it's got to be done."

"No—is that so? Oh come, now—lemme just try. Only just a little—I'd let *you*, if you was me, Tom."

"Ben, I'd like to, honest injun; but aunt Polly—well Jim wanted to do it, but she wouldn't let him; Sid wanted to do it, and she wouldn't let Sid. Now don't you see how I'm fixed? If you was to tackle this fence and anything was to happen to it—"

"Oh, shucks, I'll be just as careful. Now lemme try. Say—I'll give you the core of my apple."

"Well, here—. No, Ben, now don't. I'm afeard—"

"I'll give you *all* of it!"

Tom gave up the brush with reluctance in his face but alacrity in his heart. And while the late steamer "Big Missouri" worked and sweated in the sun, the retired artist sat on a barrel in the shade close by, dangled his legs, munched his apple, and planned the slaughter of more innocents. There was no lack of material; boys happened along every little while; they came to jeer, but remained to whitewash. By the time Ben was fagged out, Tom had traded the next chance to Billy Fisher for a kite, in good repair; and when *he* played out Johnny Miller bought in for a dead rat and a string to swing it with—and so on, and so on, hour after hour. And when the middle of the afternoon came, from being a poor poverty-stricken boy in the morning, Tom was literally rolling in wealth. He had, beside the things before mentioned, twelve marbles, part of a jewsharp, a piece of blue bottle-glass to look through, a spool cannon, a key that wouldn't unlock anything, a fragment of chalk, a glass stopper of a decanter, a tin soldier, a couple of tadpoles, six fire-crackers, a kitten with only one eye, a brass door-knob, a dog collar—but no dog—the handle of a knife, four pieces of orange peel, and a dilapidated old window sash.

He had had a nice, good, idle time all the while—plenty of company—and the fence had three coats of whitewash on it! If he hadn't run out of whitewash, he would have bankrupted every boy in the village.

Tom said to himself that it was not such a hollow world, after all. He had discovered a great law of human action, without knowing it—namely, that in order to make a man or a boy covet a thing, it is only necessary to make the thing difficult to attain. If he had been a great and wise philosopher, like the writer of this book, he would now have comprehended that Work consists of whatever a body is *obliged* to do and that Play consists of whatever a body is not obliged to do. And this would help him to understand why constructing artificial flowers or performing on a treadmill is work, while rolling ten-pins or climbing Mont Blanc is only amusement. There are wealthy gentlemen in England who drive four-horse passenger-coaches twenty or thirty miles on a daily line, in the summer, because the privilege costs them considerable money; but if they were offered wages for the service, that would turn it into work and then they would resign.

The boy mused a while over the substantial change which had taken place in his worldly circumstances, and then wended toward head-quarters to report. . . .

(from The Adventures of Tom Sawyer, *1876, chapters 2–3)*

The Prodigy

The day after reaping a rich harvest of booty from the boys who have whitewashed his aunt's fence, Tom Sawyer goes to Sunday school. Before entering the church, he accosts another boy and launches another brilliant plan that enables him to amass enough "tickets" to earn a prize in Sunday School.

"Say, Billy, got a yaller ticket?"

"Yes."

"What'll you take for her?"

"What'll you give?"

"Piece of lickrish and a fish-hook."

"Less see 'em."

Tom exhibited. They were satisfactory, and the property changed hands. Then Tom traded a couple of white alleys for three red tickets, and some small trifle or other for a couple of blue ones. He waylaid other boys as they came, and went on buying tickets of various colors ten or fifteen minutes longer. He entered the church, now, with a swarm of clean and noisy boys and girls, proceeded to his seat and started a quarrel with the first boy that came handy. The teacher, a grave, elderly man, interfered; then turned his back a moment and Tom pulled a boy's hair in the next bench, and was absorbed in his book when the boy turned around; stuck a pin in another boy, presently, in order to hear him say "Ouch!" and got a new reprimand from his teacher. Tom's whole class were of a pattern—restless, noisy, and troublesome. When they came to recite their lessons, not one of them knew his verses perfectly, but had to be prompted all along. However, they worried through, and each got his reward—in small blue tickets, each with a passage of Scripture on it; each blue ticket was pay for two verses of the recitation. Ten blue tickets equaled a red one, and could be exchanged for it; ten red tickets equaled a yellow one; for ten yellow tickets the Superintendent gave a very plainly bound Bible, (worth forty cents in those easy times,) to the pupil. How many of my readers would have the industry and the application to memorize two thousand verses, even for a Dore Bible? And yet Mary had acquired two Bibles in this way—it was the patient work of two years—and a boy of German parentage had won four or five. He once recited three thousand verses without stopping; but the strain upon his mental faculties was too great, and he was little better than an idiot from that day forth—a grievous misfortune for the school, for on great occasions, before company, the Superintendent (as Tom expressed it) had always made this boy come out and "spread himself." Only the older pupils managed to keep their tickets and stick to their tedious work long enough to get a Bible, and so the delivery of one of these prizes was a rare and noteworthy circumstance; the successful pupil was so great and conspicuous for that day that on the spot every scholar's breast was fired with a fresh ambition that often lasted a couple of weeks. It is possible that Tom's mental stomach had never really hungered for one of those prizes, but unquestionably his entire being had for many a day longed for the glory and the éclat that came with it. . . .

When Judge Thatcher visits the Sunday School, the instructor grows anxious to show off a "prodigy" from among his pupils.

There was only one thing wanting, to make Mr. Walters' ecstacy complete, and that was a chance to deliver a Bible-prize and exhibit a prodigy. Several pupils had a few yellow tickets, but none had enough—he had been around among the star pupils inquiring. He would have given worlds, now, to have that German lad back again with a sound mind.

And now at this moment, when hope was dead, Tom Sawyer came forward with nine yellow tickets, nine red tickets, and ten blue ones, and demanded a Bible. This was a thunderbolt out of a clear sky. Walters was not expecting an application from this source for the next ten years. But there was no getting around it—here were the certified checks, and they were good for their face. Tom was therefore elevated to a place with the Judge and the other elect, and the great news was announced from head-quarters. It was the most stunning surprise of the decade, and so profound was the sensation that it lifted the new hero up to the judicial one's altitude, and the school had two marvels to gaze upon in place of one. The boys were all eaten up with envy—but those that suffered the bitterest pangs were those who perceived too late that they themselves had contributed to this hated splendor by trading tickets to Tom for the wealth he had amassed in selling white-washing privileges. These despised themselves, as being the dupes of a wily fraud, a guileful snake in the grass.

The prize was delivered to Tom with as much effusion as the Superintendent could pump up under the circumstances; but it lacked somewhat of the true gush, for the poor fellow's instinct taught him that there was a mystery here that could not well bear the light, perhaps; it was simply preposterous that *this* boy had warehoused two thousand sheaves of Scriptural wisdom on his premises—a dozen would strain his capacity, without a doubt. . . .

Tom was introduced to the Judge; but his tongue was tied, his breath would hardly come, his heart quaked—partly because of the awful greatness of the man, but mainly because he was *her* parent. He would have liked to fall down and worship him, if it were in the dark. The Judge put his hand on Tom's head and called him a fine little man, and asked him what his name was. The boy stammered, gasped, and got it out:

"Tom."

"Oh, no, not Tom—it is—"

"Thomas."

"Ah, that's it. I thought there was more to it, maybe. That's very well. But you've another one I daresay, and you'll tell it to me, won't you?"

"Tell the gentleman your other name, Thomas," said Walters, "and say *sir.*—You mustn't forget your manners."

"Thomas Sawyer—sir."

"That's it! That's a good boy. Fine boy. Fine, manly little fellow. Two thousand verses is a great many—very, very great many. And you never can be sorry for the trouble you took to learn them; for knowledge is worth more than anything there is in the world; it's what makes great men and good men; you'll be a great man and a good man yourself, some day, Thomas, and then you'll look back and say, It's all owing to the precious Sunday-school privileges of my boyhood—it's all owing to my dear teachers that taught me to learn—it's all owing to the good Superintendent, who encouraged me, and watched over me, and gave me a beautiful Bible—a splendid elegant Bible, to keep and have it all for my own, always—it's all owing to right bringing up! That is what you will say, Thomas—and you wouldn't take any money for those two thousand verses—no indeed you wouldn't. And now you wouldn't mind telling me and this lady some of the things you've learned—no, I know you wouldn't—for we are proud of little boys that learn. Now no doubt you know the names of all the twelve disciples. Won't you tell us the names of the first two that were appointed?"

Tom was tugging at a button and looking sheepish. He blushed, now, and his eyes fell. Mr. Walters' heart sank within him. He said to himself, it is not possible that the boy can answer the simplest question—why *did* the Judge ask him? Yet he felt obliged to speak up and say:

"Answer the gentleman, Thomas—don't be afraid."

Tom still hung fire.

"Now I know you'll tell *me*," said the lady. "The names of the first two disciples were—"

"DAVID AND GOLIAH!"

Let us draw the curtain of charity over the rest of the scene.

(from The Adventures of Tom Sawyer, *1876, chapter 4)*

Tom Sawyer's Bloodthirsty Gang

Early in Adventures of Huckleberry Finn, *Huck (the narrator) accompanies Tom Sawyer and other boys to the limestone cave south of St. Petersburg. After Tom makes all the boys swear to secrecy, they enter the cave through a hidden opening. Inside the cave, Tom opens the meeting:*

"*N*ow we'll start this band of robbers and call it Tom Sawyer's Gang. Everybody that wants to join has got to take an oath, and write his name in blood."

Everybody was willing. So Tom got out a sheet of paper that he had wrote the oath on, and read it. It swore every boy to stick to the band, and never tell any of the secrets; and if anybody done anything to any boy in the band, whichever boy was ordered to kill that person and his family must do it, and he mustn't eat and he mustn't sleep till he had killed them and hacked a cross in their breasts, which was the sign of the band. And nobody that didn't belong to the band could use that mark, and if he did he must be sued; and if he done it again he must be killed. And if anybody that belonged to the band told the secrets, he must have his throat cut, and then have his carcass burnt up and the ashes scattered all around, and his name blotted off the list with blood and never mentioned again by the gang, but have a curse put on it and be forgot, forever.

Everybody said it was a real beautiful oath, and asked Tom if he got it out of his own head. He said some of it, but the rest was out of pirate books and robber books, and every gang that was high-toned had it.

Some thought it would be good to kill the *families* of boys that told the secrets. Tom said it was a good idea, so he took a pencil and wrote it in. Then Ben Rogers says:

"Here's Huck Finn, he hain't got no family—what you going to do 'bout him?"

"Well, hain't he got a father?" says Tom Sawyer.

"Yes, he's got a father, but you can't never find him these days. He used to lay drunk with the hogs in the tanyard, but he hain't been seen in these parts for a year or more."

They talked it over, and they was going to rule me out, because they said every boy must have a family or somebody to kill, or else it wouldn't be fair and square for the others. Well, nobody could think of anything to do—everybody was stumped, and set still. I was most ready to cry; but all at once I thought of a way, and so I offered them Miss Watson—they could kill her. Everybody said:

"Oh, she'll do, she'll do. That's all right. Huck can come in."

Then they all stuck a pin in their fingers to get blood to sign with, and I made my mark on the paper.

"Now," says Ben Rogers, "what's the line of business of this Gang?"

"Nothing only robbery and murder," Tom said.

"But who are we going to rob? houses—or cattle—or—"

"Stuff! stealing cattle and such things ain't robbery; it's burglary," says Tom Sawyer. "We ain't burglars. That ain't no sort of style. We are highwaymen. We stop stages and carriages on the road, with masks on, and kill the people and take their watches and money."

"Must we always kill the people?"

"Oh, certainly. It's best. Some authorities think different, but mostly it's considered best to kill them. Except some that you bring to the cave here and keep them till they're ransomed."

"Ransomed? What's that?"

"I don't know. But that's what they do. I've seen it in books; and so of course that's what we've got to do."

"But how can we do it if we don't know what it is?"

"Why, blame it all, we've *got* to do it. Don't I tell you it's in the books? Do you want to go to doing different from what's in the books, and get things all muddled up?"

"Oh, that's all very fine to *say*, Tom Sawyer, but how in the nation are these fellows going to be ransomed if we don't know how to do it to them?—that's the thing *I* want to get at. Now, what do you *reckon* it is?"

"Well, I don't know. But per'aps if we keep them till they're ransomed, it means that we keep them till they're dead."

"Now, that's something *like*. That'll answer. Why couldn't you said that before? We'll keep them till they're ransomed to death; and a bothersome lot they'll be, too, eating up everything and always trying to get loose."

"How you talk, Ben Rogers. How can they get loose when there's a guard over them, ready to shoot them down if they move a peg?"

"A guard. Well, that *is* good. So somebody's got to set up all night and never get any sleep, just so as to watch them. I think that's foolishness. Why can't a body take a club and ransom them as soon as they get here?"

"Because it ain't in the books—that's why. Now, Ben Rogers, do you want to do things regular, or don't you?— that's the idea. Don't you reckon that the people that made the books knows what's the correct thing to do? Do you reckon *you* can learn 'em anything? Not by a good deal. No, sir, we'll just go on and ransom them in the regular way."

"All right. I don't mind; but I say it's a fool way, anyhow. Say—do we kill the women, too?"

"Well, Ben Rogers, if I was as ignorant as you I wouldn't let on. Kill the women? No—nobody ever saw anything in the books like that. You fetch them to the cave, and you're always as polite as pie to them; and by-and-by they fall in love with you and never want to go home any more."

"Well, if that's the way, I'm agreed, but I don't take no stock in it. Mighty soon we'll have the cave so cluttered up with women, and fellows waiting to be ransomed, that there won't be no place for the robbers. But go ahead, I ain't got nothing to say."

Little Tommy Barnes was asleep now, and when they waked him up he was scared, and cried, and said he wanted to go home to his ma, and didn't want to be a robber any more.

So they all made fun of him, and called him cry-baby, and that made him mad, and he said he would go straight and tell all the secrets. But Tom give him five cents to keep quiet, and said we would all go home and meet next week and rob somebody and kill some people.

Ben Rogers said he couldn't get out much, only Sundays, and so he wanted to begin next Sunday; but all the boys said it would be wicked to do it on Sunday, and that settled the thing. They agreed to get together and fix a day as soon as they could, and then we elected Tom Sawyer first captain and Joe Harper second captain of the Gang, and so started home.

I clumb up the shed and crept into my window just before day was breaking. My new clothes was all greased up and clayey, and I was dog-tired.

. . . We played robber now and then about a month, and then I resigned. All the boys did. We hadn't robbed nobody, we hadn't killed any people, but only just pretended. We used to hop out of the woods and go charging down on hog-drovers and women in carts taking garden stuff to market, but we never hived any of them. Tom Sawyer called the hogs "ingots," and he called the turnips and stuff "julery," and we would go to the cave and pow-wow over what we had done and how many people we had killed and marked. But I couldn't see no profit in it. One time Tom sent a boy to run about town with a blazing stick, which he called a slogan (which was the sign for the Gang to get together), and then he said he had got secret news by his spies that next day a whole parcel of Spanish merchants and rich A-rabs was going to camp in Cave Hollow with two hundred elephants, and six hundred camels, and over a thousand "sumter" mules, all loaded down with di'monds, and they didn't have only a guard of four hundred soldiers, and so we would lay in ambuscade,

as he called it, and kill the lot and scoop the things. He said
we must slick up our swords and guns, and get ready. He never
could go after even a turnip-cart but he must have the swords
and guns all scoured up for it; though they was only lath and
broom-sticks, and you might scour at them till you rotted and
then they warn't worth a mouthful of ashes more than what
they was before. I didn't believe we could lick such a crowd
of Spaniards and A-rabs, but I wanted to see the camels and
elephants, so I was on hand next day, Saturday, in the ambuscade; and when we got the word, we rushed out of the woods
and down the hill. But there warn't no Spaniards and A-rabs,
and there warn't no camels nor no elephants. It warn't anything but a Sunday-school picnic, and only a primer class at
that. We busted it up, and chased the children up the hollow;
but we never got anything but some doughnuts and jam,
though Ben Rogers got a rag doll, and Joe Harper got a hymn-
book and a tract; and then the teacher charged in and made
us drop everything and cut. I didn't see no di'monds, and I
told Tom Sawyer so. He said there was loads of them there,
anyway; and he said there was A-rabs there, too, and elephants and things. I said, why couldn't we see them, then?
He said if I warn't so ignorant, but had read a book called
Don Quixote, I would know without asking. He said it was all
done by enchantment. He said there was hundreds of soldiers
there, and elephants and treasure, and so on, but we had ene-
mies which he called magicians, and they had turned the

whole thing into an infant Sunday-school, just out of spite. I said, all right, then the thing for us to do was to go for the magicians. Tom Sawyer said I was a numskull. . . .

After Tom explains that rubbing an old tin lamp will call up a genie, Huck tries following this advice.

I thought all this over for two or three days, and then I reckoned I would see if there was anything in it. I got an old tin lamp and an iron ring, and went out in the woods and rubbed and rubbed till I sweat like an Injun, calculating to build a palace and sell it; but it warn't no use, none of the genies come. So then I judged that all that stuff was only just one of Tom Sawyer's lies. I reckoned he believed in the A-rabs and the elephants, but as for me I think different. It had all the marks of a Sunday-school.

(from Adventures of Huckleberry Finn, *1884, chapters 2–3)*

What Becomes of
Good Children

*Let us endeavor so to live that when we come to die
even the undertaker will be sorry.*

*Make it a point to do something every day that you
don't want to do. This is the golden rule for acquiring
the habit of doing your duty without pain.*

*All good things arrive unto them that wait—
and don't die in the meantime.*

Model Boys

*When Mark Twain revisited his boyhood home at Hannibal,
Missouri, in 1882, he attended a Sunday school meeting,
where he looked for the "model boy."*

The Model Boy of my time—we never had but the one—was
perfect: perfect in manners, perfect in dress, perfect in conduct, perfect in filial piety, perfect in exterior godliness; but
at bottom he was a prig; and as for the contents of his skull,
they could have changed place with the contents of a pie and
nobody would have been the worse off for it but the pie. This
fellow's reproachlessness was a standing reproach to every lad
in the village. He was the admiration of all the mothers, and
the detestation of all their sons. I was told what became of
him, but as it was a disappointment to me, I will not enter
into details. He succeeded in life.

(from Life on the Mississippi, *1883, chapter 54)*

Mark Twain never regarded himself as a model boy; however, he did have an inflated opinion of his youthful virtues.

$\mathcal{N}$ow, I recall that when I was a boy I was a good boy—I was a very good boy. Why, I was the best boy in my school. I was the best boy in that little Mississippi town where I lived. The population was only about twenty million. You may not believe it, but I was the best boy in that state—and in the United States, for that matter.

But I don't know why I never heard anyone say that but myself. I always recognized it. But even those nearest and dearest to me couldn't seem to see it. My mother, especially, seemed to think there was something wrong with that estimate. And she never got over that prejudice.

Now, when my mother got to be eighty-five years old her memory failed her. She forgot little threads that hold life's patches of meaning together. She was living out West then, and I went on to visit her.

I hadn't seen my mother in a year or so. And when I got there she knew my face, knew I was married, knew I had a family and that I was living with them. But she couldn't, for the life of her, tell my name or who I was. So I told her I was her boy.

"But you don't live with me," she said.

"No," said I, "I'm living in Hartford."

"What are you doing there?"

"Going to school."

"Large school?"

"Very large."

"All boys?"

"All boys."

"And how do you stand?" said my mother.

"I'm the best boy in that school," I answered.

"Well," said my mother, with a return of her old fire, "I'd like to know what the other boys are like."

Now, one point in this story is the fact that my mother's mind went back to my school days, and remembered my little youthful self-prejudice when she'd forgotten everything else about me.

The other point is the moral. There's one there that you will find if you search for it.

(from a speech given in March 1906)

A Drowned Boy

The idea of being virtuous only to die young fascinated Mark Twain. In Huckleberry Finn, *Huck spends several weeks in the home of the Grangerford family, whose deceased daughter Emmeline had written poems in honor of dead children. Huck is particularly impressed by Emmeline's poem about Stephen Dowling Bots, who "fell down a well and was drowned":*

Ode to Stephen Dowling Bots, Dec'd.

And did young Stephen sicken,
  And did young Stephen die?
And did the sad hearts thicken,
  And did the mourners cry?

No; such was not the fate of
  Young Stephen Dowling Bots;
Though sad hearts round him thickened,
  'Twas not from sickness' shots.

No whooping-cough did rack his frame,
  Nor measles drear, with spots;
Not these impaired the sacred name
  Of Stephen Dowling Bots.

Despised love struck not with woe
    That head of curly knots,
Nor stomach troubles laid him low,
    Young Stephen Dowling Bots.

O no. Then list with tearful eye,
    Whilst I his fate do tell.
His soul did from this cold world fly,
    By falling down a well.

They got him out and emptied him;
    Alas it was too late;
His spirit was gone for to sport aloft
    In the realms of the good and great.

(from Adventures of Huckleberry Finn, *1884, chapter 17)*

The Story of the Good Little Boy
Who Did Not Prosper

This story, first published in 1870, sums up Mark Twain's feelings about the futility of being good. He wrote it as a companion piece to his earlier story, "The Bad Little Boy Who Did Not Come to Grief."

Once there was a good little boy by the name of Jacob Blivens. He always obeyed his parents, no matter how absurd and unreasonable their demands were; and he always learned his book, and never was late at Sabbath-school. He would not play hookey, even when his sober judgment told him it was the most profitable thing he could do. None of the other boys could ever make that boy out, he acted so strangely. He wouldn't lie, no matter how convenient it was. He just said it was wrong to lie, and that was sufficient for him. And he was so honest that he was simply ridiculous. The curious ways that that Jacob had, surpassed everything. He wouldn't play marbles on Sunday, he wouldn't rob birds' nests, he wouldn't give hot pennies to organ-grinders' monkeys; he didn't seem to take any interest in any kind of rational amusement. So the other boys used to try to reason it out and come to an understanding of him, but they couldn't arrive at any satisfactory conclusion. As I said before, they could only figure out a sort of vague idea that he was "afflicted," and so they took him under their protection, and never allowed any harm to come to him.

This good little boy read all the Sunday-school books; they were his greatest delight. This was the whole secret of it. He believed in the good little boys they put in the Sunday-school books; he had every confidence in them. He longed to come across one of them alive, once, but he never did. They all died before his time, maybe. Whenever he read about a particularly good one he turned over quickly to the end to see what became of him, because he wanted to travel thousands of miles and gaze on him; but it wasn't any use; that good little boy always died in the last chapter, and there was a picture of the funeral, with all his relations and the Sunday-school children standing around the grave in pantaloons that were too short, and bonnets that were too large, and everybody crying into handkerchiefs that had as much as a yard and a half of stuff in them. He was always headed off in this way. He never could see one of those good little boys on account of his always dying in the last chapter.

Jacob had a noble ambition to be put in a Sunday-school book. He wanted to be put in, with pictures representing him gloriously declining to lie to his mother, and her weeping for joy about it; and pictures representing him standing on the doorstep giving a penny to a poor beggar-woman with six children, and telling her to spend it freely, but not to be extravagant, because extravagance is a sin; and pictures of him magnanimously refusing to tell on the bad boy who always lay in wait for him around the corner as he came from school, and welted him over the head with a lath, and then chased him home, saying, "Hi! hi!" as he proceeded. This was the ambition of young Jacob Blivens. He wished to be put in a Sunday-school book. It made him feel a little uncomfortable sometimes when he reflected that the good little boys always died. He loved to live, you know, and this was the most unpleasant feature about being a Sunday-school-book boy. He knew it was not healthy to be good. He knew it was more fatal than consumption to be so supernaturally good as the boys in the books were; he knew that none of them had been able to stand it long, and it pained him to think that if they put him in a book he wouldn't ever see it, or even if they did get the book out before he died it wouldn't be popular without any picture of his funeral in the back part of it. It couldn't be much of a Sunday-school book that couldn't tell about the advice he gave to the community when he was dying. So at last, of course, he had to make up his mind to do the best he could under the circumstances—to live right, and hang on as long as he could, and have his dying speech all ready when his time came.

But somehow nothing ever went right with this good little boy; nothing ever turned out with him the way it turned out with the good little boys in the books. They always had a good time, and the bad boys had the broken legs; but in his case there was a screw loose somewhere; and it all happened just the other way. When he found Jim Blake stealing apples, and went under the tree to read to him about the bad little boy who fell out of a neighbor's apple-tree and broke his arm, Jim fell out of the tree too, but he fell on *him*, and broke *his* arm, and Jim wasn't hurt at all. Jacob couldn't understand that. There wasn't anything in the books like it.

And once, when some bad boys pushed a blind man over in the mud, and Jacob ran to help him up and receive his blessing, the blind man did not give him any blessing at all, but whacked him over the head with his stick and said he would like to catch him shoving *him* again, and then pretending to help him up. This was not in accordance with any of the books. Jacob looked them all over to see.

One thing that Jacob wanted to do was to find a lame dog that hadn't any place to stay, and was hungry and persecuted, and bring him home and pet him and have that dog's imperishable gratitude. And at last he found one and was happy; and he brought him home and fed him, but when he was going to pet him the dog flew at him and tore all the clothes off him except those that were in front, and made a spectacle of him that was astonishing. He examined authorities, but he could not understand the matter. It was of the same breed of dogs that was in the books, but it acted very differently. Whatever this boy did he got into trouble. The very things the boys in the books got rewarded for turned out to be about the most unprofitable things he could invest in.

Once, when he was on his way to Sunday-school, he saw some bad boys starting off pleasuring in a sailboat. He was filled with consternation, because he knew from his reading that boys who went sailing on Sunday invariably got drowned. So he ran out on a raft to warn them, but a log turned with him and slid him into the river. A man got him out pretty soon, and the doctor pumped the water out of him, and gave him a fresh start with his bellows, but he caught cold and lay sick a-bed nine weeks. But the most unaccountable thing about it was that the bad boys in the boat had a good time all day, and then reached home alive and well in the most surprising manner. Jacob Blivens said there was nothing like these things in the books. He was perfectly dumbfounded.

When he got well he was a little discouraged, but he resolved to keep on trying anyhow. He knew that so far his experience wouldn't do to go in a book, but he hadn't yet reached the allotted term of life for good little boys, and he hoped to be able to make a record yet if he could hold on till his time was fully up. If everything else failed he had his dying speech to fall back on.

He examined his authorities, and found that it was now time for him to go to sea as a cabin-boy. He called on a ship captain and made his application, and when the captain asked for his recommendations he proudly drew out a tract and pointed to the words. "To Jacob Blivens, from his affectionate teacher." But the captain was a coarse, vulgar man, and he said, "Oh, that be blowed! *that* wasn't any proof that he know how to wash dishes or handle a slush-bucket, and he guessed he didn't want him." This was altogether the most extraordinary thing that ever happened to Jacob in all his life. A compliment from a teacher, on a tract, had never failed to move the tenderest emotions of ship captains, and open the way to all offices of honor and profit in their gift—it never had in any book that ever he had read. He could hardly believe his senses.

This boy always had a hard time of it. Nothing ever came out according to the authorities with him. At last, one day, when he was around hunting up bad little boys to admonish, he found a lot of them in the old iron foundry fixing up a little joke on fourteen or fifteen dogs, which they had tied together in long procession, and were going to ornament with empty nitro-glycerine cans made fast to their tails. Jacob's heart was touched. He sat down on one of those cans (for he never minded grease when duty was before him), and he took hold of the foremost dog by the collar, and turned his reproving eye upon wicked Tom Jones. But just at that moment Alderman McWelter, full of wrath, stepped in. All the bad boys ran away, but Jacob Blivens rose in conscious innocence and began one of those stately little Sunday-school-book speeches which always commence with "Oh, sir!" in dead opposition to the fact that no boy, good or bad, ever starts a remark with "Oh, sir." But the alderman never waited to hear the rest. He took Jacob Blivens by the ear and turned him around, and hit him a whack in the rear with the flat of his hand; and in an instant that good little boy shot out through the roof and soared away towards the sun, with the fragments of those fifteen dogs stringing after him like the tail of a kite.

And there wasn't a sign of that alderman or that old iron foundry left on the face of the earth; and, as for young Jacob Blivens, he never got a chance to make his last dying speech after all his trouble fixing it up, unless he made it to the birds; because, although the bulk of him came down all right in a tree-top in an adjoining county, the rest of him was apportioned around among four townships, and so they had to hold five inquests on him to find out whether he was dead or not, and how it occurred. You never saw a boy scattered so.

Thus perished the good little boy who did the best he could, but didn't come out according to the books. Every boy who ever did as he did prospered except him. His case is truly remarkable. It will probably never be accounted for.

(First published under the same title in Galaxy, *May 1870)*

What Becomes of
Bad Children

Do your duty today and repent tomorrow.

Be good and you will be lonely.

A Tonic to His Mother

Mark Twain's recollections of his boyhood and his occasionally
tumultuous relationship with his mother often read like
chapters out of Tom Sawyer.

*M*y mother had a good deal of trouble with me, but I think
she enjoyed it. She had none at all with my brother Henry,
who was two years younger than I, and I think that the unbro-
ken monotony of his goodness and truthfulness and obedi-
ence would have been a burden to her but for the relief and
variety which I furnished in the other direction. I was a tonic.
I was valuable to her. I never thought of it before, but now I
see it. I never knew Henry to do a vicious thing toward me,
or toward anyone else—but he frequently did righteous ones
that cost me as heavily. It was his duty to report me, when I
needed reporting and neglected to do it myself, and he was
very faithful in discharging that duty. He is Sid in Tom
Sawyer. But Sid was not Henry. Henry was a very much finer
and better boy than ever Sid was.

It was Henry who called my mother's attention to the fact
that the thread with which she had sewed my collar together
to keep me from going in swimming had changed color. My
mother would not have discovered it but for that, and she was
manifestly piqued when she recognized that that prominent
bit of circumstantial evidence had escaped her sharp eye.
That detail probably added a detail to my punishment. It is

human. We generally visit our shortcomings on somebody else when there is a possible excuse for it—but no matter. I took it out of Henry. There is always compensation for such as are unjustly used. I often took it out of him—sometimes as an advance payment for something which I hadn't yet done. These were occasions when the opportunity was too strong a temptation, and I had to draw on the future. I did not need to copy this idea from my mother, and probably didn't. It is most likely that I invented it for myself. Still, she wrought upon that principle upon occasion.

If the incident of the broken sugar bowl is in "Tom Sawyer"—I don't remember whether it is or not—that is an example of it. Henry never stole sugar. He took it openly from the bowl. His mother knew he wouldn't take sugar when she wasn't looking, but she had her doubts about me. Not exactly doubts, either. She knew very well I *would*. One day when she was not present Henry took sugar from her prized and precious old-English sugar bowl, which was an heirloom in the family—and he managed to break the bowl. It was the first time I had ever had a chance to tell anything on him, and I was inexpressibly glad. I told him I was going to tell on him, but he was not disturbed. When my mother came in and saw the bowl lying on the floor in fragments, she was speechless for a minute. I allowed that silence to work; I judged it would increase the effect. I was waiting for her to ask, "Who did that?"—so that I could fetch out my news. But it was an error of calculation. When she got through with her silence she didn't ask anything about it—she merely gave me a crack on the skull with her thimble that I felt all the way down to my heels. Then I broke out with my injured innocence, expecting to make her very sorry that she had punished the wrong one. I expected her to do something remorseful and pathetic. I told her that I was not the one—it was Henry. But there was no upheaval. She said, without emotion: "It's all right. It isn't any matter. You deserve it for something you've done that I didn't know about; and if you haven't done it, why then you deserve it for something that you are going to do that I shan't hear about."

There was a stairway outside the house, which led up to the rear part of the second story. One day Henry was sent on an errand, and he took a tin bucket along. I knew he would have to ascend those stairs, so I went up and locked the door on the inside, and came down into the garden, which had been newly plowed and was rich in choice, firm clods of black mold. I gathered a generous equipment of these and ambushed him. I waited till he had climbed the stairs and was near the landing and couldn't escape. Then I bombarded him with clods, which he warded off with his tin bucket the best he could, but without much success, for I was a good marksman. The clods smashing against the weather-boarding fetched my mother out to see what was the matter, and I tried to explain that I was amusing Henry. Both of them were after me in a minute, but I knew the way over that high board fence and escaped for that time. After an hour or two, when I ventured back, there was no one around and I thought the incident was closed. But it was not so. Henry was ambushing me. With an unusually competent aim for him, he landed a stone on the side of my head which raised a bump there which felt like the Matterhorn. I carried it to my mother straightway for sympathy, but she was not strongly moved. It seemed to be her idea that incidents like this would eventually reform me if I harvested enough of them. So the matter was only educational. I had had a sterner view of it than that before.

(from his autobiography)

The Story of the Bad Little Boy Who Didn't Come to Grief

In rebelling against the goody-goody boys who populated the children's books on which he was raised, Mark Twain relished turning moralistic tales upside-down in this story.

Once there was a bad little boy whose name was Jim—though, if you will notice, you will find that bad little boys are nearly always called James in your Sunday-school books. It was strange, but still it was true that this one was called Jim.

He didn't have any sick mother, either—a sick mother who
was pious and had the consumption, and would be glad to lie
down in the grave and be at rest, but for the strong love she
bore her boy, and the anxiety she felt that the world might be
harsh and cold towards him when she was gone. Most bad
boys in the Sunday-books are named James, and have sick
mothers, who teach them to say, "Now, I lay me down," etc.,
and sing them to sleep with sweet, plaintive voices, and then
kiss them good-night, and kneel down by the bedside and
weep. But it was different with this fellow. He was named
Jim, and there wasn't anything the matter with his mother—
no consumption, nor anything of that kind. She was rather
stout than otherwise, and she was not pious; moreover, she
was not anxious on Jim's account. She said if he were to break
his neck it wouldn't be much loss. She always spanked Jim to
sleep, and she never kissed him good-night; on the contrary,
she boxed his ears when she was ready to leave him.

Once, this little bad boy stole the key of the pantry, and
slipped in there and helped himself to some jam, and filled
up the vessel with tar, so that his mother would never know
the difference; but all at once a terrible feeling didn't come
over him, and something didn't seem to whisper to him, "Is
it right to disobey my mother? Isn't it sinful to do this? Where
do bad little boys go who gobble up their good kind mother's
jam?" and then he didn't kneel down all alone and promise
never to be wicked any more, and rise up with a light, happy
heart, and go and tell his mother all about it, and beg her for-

giveness, and be blessed by her with tears of pride and thankfulness in her eyes. No; that is the way with all other bad boys in the books; but it happened otherwise with this Jim, strangely enough. He ate that jam, and said it was bully, in his sinful, vulgar way; and he put in the tar, and said that was bully also, and laughed, and observed "that the old woman would get up and snort" when she found it out; and when she did find it out, he denied knowing anything about it, and she whipped him severely, and he did the crying himself. Everything about this boy was curious—everything turned out differently with him from the way it does to the bad James in the books.

Once he climbed up in Farmer Acorn's apple-tree to steal apples, and the limb didn't break, and he didn't fall and break his arm, and get torn by the farmer's great dog, and then languish on a sick bed for weeks, and repent and become good. Oh! no; he stole as many apples as he wanted and came down all right; and he was all ready for the dog too, and knocked him endways with a brick when he came to tear him. It was very strange—nothing like it ever happened in those mild little books with marbled backs, and with pictures in them of men with swallow-tailed coats and bell-crowned hats, and pantaloons that are short in the legs, and women with the waists of their dresses under their arms, and no hoops on. Nothing like it in any of the Sunday-school books.

Once he stole the teacher's pen-knife, and, when he was afraid it would be found out and he would get whipped, he slipped it into George Wilson's cap—poor Widow Wilson's son, the moral boy, the good little boy of the village, who always obeyed his mother, and never told an untruth, and was fond of his lessons, and infatuated with Sunday-school. And when the knife dropped from the cap, and poor George hung his head and blushed, as if in conscious guilt, and the grieved teacher charged the theft upon him, and was just in the very act of bringing the switch down upon his trembling shoulders, a white-haired improbable justice of the peace did not suddenly appear in their midst, and strike an attitude and say, "Spare this noble boy—there stands the cowering culprit! I was passing the school-door at recess, and unseen myself, I saw the theft committed!" And then Jim didn't get whaled, and the venerable justice didn't read the tearful school a homily and take George by the hand and say such a boy deserved to be exalted, and then tell him to come and make his home with him, and sweep out the office, and make fires, and run errands, and chop wood, and study law, and help his wife to do household labors, and have all the balance of the time to play, and get forty cents a month, and be happy. No; it would have happened that way in the books, but it didn't happen that way to Jim. No meddling old clam of a justice dropped in to make trouble, and so the model boy George got thrashed, and Jim was glad of it because, you know, Jim hated moral boys. Jim said he was "down on them milk-sops." Such was the coarse language of this bad, neglected boy.

But the strangest thing that ever happened to Jim was the time he went boating on Sunday, and didn't get drowned, and that other time that he got caught out in the storm when he was fishing on Sunday, and didn't get struck by lightning. Why, you might look, and look, all through the Sunday-school books from now till next Christmas, and you would never come across anything like this. Oh no; you would find that all the bad boys who go boating on Sunday invariably get drowned; and all the bad boys who get caught out in storms when they are fishing on Sunday infallibly get struck by lightning. Boats with bad boys in them always upset on Sunday, and it always storms when bad boys go fishing on the Sabbath. How this Jim ever escaped is a mystery to me.

This Jim bore a charmed life—that must have been the way of it. Nothing could hurt him. He even gave the elephant in the menagerie a plug of tobacco, and the elephant didn't knock the top of his head off with his trunk. He browsed around the cupboard after essence of peppermint, and didn't make a mistake and drink *aqua fortis*. He stole his father's gun and went hunting on the Sabbath, and didn't shoot three or four of his fingers off. He struck his little sister on the temple with his fist when he was angry, and she didn't linger in pain through long summer days, and die with sweet words of forgiveness upon her lips that redoubled the anguish of his breaking heart. No; she got over it. He ran off and went to sea at last, and didn't come back and find himself sad and alone in the world, his loved ones sleeping in the quiet church-yard, and the vine-embowered home of his boyhood tumbled down and gone to decay. Ah! no; he came home as drunk as a piper, and got into the station-house the first thing.

And he grew up and married, and raised a large family, and brained them all with an axe one night, and got wealthy by all manner of cheating and rascality; and now he is the infernalest wickedest scoundrel in his native village, and is universally respected, and belongs to the Legislature.

So you see there never was a bad James in the Sunday-school books that had such a streak of luck as this sinful Jim with the charmed life.

> *(Originally published in the* Californian *[December 23, 1865] as "The Christmas Fireside")*

Edward Mills and George Benton: A Tale

Mark Twain's feelings about what fates good and bad boys will most likely experience are neatly summed up in this moralistic tale about adoptive brothers.

These two were distantly related to each other—seventh cousins, or something of that sort. While still babies they became orphans, and were adopted by the Brants, a childless couple, who quickly grew very fond of them. The Brants were always saying:

> Be pure, honest, sober, industrious,
> and considerate of others, and
> success in life is assured.

The children heard this repeated some thousands of times before they understood it; they could repeat it themselves long before they could say the Lord's Prayer; it was painted over the nursery door, and was about the first thing they learned to read. It was destined to become the unswerving rule of Edward Mills's life. Sometimes the Brants changed the wording a little, and said:

> Be pure, honest, sober, industrious,
> considerate, and you will never lack
> friends.

Baby Mills was a comfort to everybody about him. When he wanted candy and could not have it, he listened to reason, and contented himself without it. When Baby Benton wanted candy, he cried for it until he got it. Baby Mills took care of his toys; Baby Benton always destroyed his in a very brief time, and then made himself so insistently disagreeable that, in order to have peace in the house, little Edward was persuaded to yield up his playthings to him.

When the children were a little older, Georgie became a heavy expense in one respect: he took no care of his clothes; consequently, he shone frequently in new ones, which was not the case with Eddie. The boys grew apace. Eddie was an increasing comfort, Georgie an increasing solicitude. It was always sufficient to say, in answer to Eddie's petitions, "I would rather you would not do it"—meaning swimming, skating, picnicking, berrying, circusing, and all sorts of things which boys delight in. But *no* answer was sufficient for Georgie; he had to be humored in his desires, or he would carry them with a high hand. Naturally, no boy got more swimming, skating, berrying, and so forth than he; no boy ever had a better time. The good Brants did not allow the boys to play out after nine in summer evenings; they were sent to bed at that hour; Eddie honorably remained, but Georgie usually slipped out of the window toward ten, and enjoyed himself till midnight. It seemed impossible to break Georgie of this bad habit, but the Brants managed it at last by hiring him, with apples and marbles, to stay in. The good Brants gave all their time and attention to vain endeavors to regulate Georgie; they said, with grateful tears in their eyes, that Eddie needed no efforts of theirs, he was so good, so considerate, and in all ways so perfect.

By and by the boys were big enough to work, so they were apprenticed to a trade: Edward went voluntarily; George was coaxed and bribed. Edward worked hard and faithfully, and ceased to be an expense to the good Brants; they praised him, so did his master; but George ran away, and it cost Mr. Brant both money and trouble to hunt him up and get him back. By and by he ran away again—more money and more trouble. He ran away a third time—and stole a few little things to carry with him. Trouble and expense for Mr. Brant once more; and, besides, it was with the greatest difficulty that he succeeded in persuading the master to let the youth go unprosecuted for the theft.

Edward worked steadily along, and in time became a full partner in his master's business. George did not improve; he kept the loving hearts of his aged benefactors full of trouble, and their hands full of inventive activities to protect him from ruin. Edward, as a boy, had interested himself in Sunday-schools, debating societies, penny missionary affairs, anti-tobacco organizations, anti-profanity associations, and all such things; as a man, he was a quiet but steady and reliable helper in the church, the temperance societies, and in all movements looking to the aiding and uplifting of men. This excited no remark, attracted no attention—for it was his "natural bent."

Finally, the old people died. The will testified their loving pride in Edward, and left their little property to George— because he "needed it"; whereas, "owing to a bountiful Providence," such was not the case with Edward. The property was left to George conditionally: he must buy out Edward's partner with it; else it must go to a benevolent organization called the Prisoner's Friend Society. The old people left a letter, in which they begged their dear son Edward to take their

place and watch over George, and help and shield him as
they had done.

Edward dutifully acquiesced, and George became his partner in the business. He was not a valuable partner: he had
been meddling with drink before; he soon developed into a
constant tippler now, and his flesh and eyes showed the fact
unpleasantly. Edward had been courting a sweet and kindly
spirited girl for some time. They loved each other dearly,
and—But about this period George began to haunt her tear-
fully and imploringly, and at last she went crying to Edward,
and said her high and holy duty was plain before her—she
must not let her own selfish desires interfere with it: she must
marry "poor George" and "reform him." It would break her
heart, she knew it would, and so on; but duty was duty. So
she married George, and Edward's heart came very near
breaking, as well as her own. However, Edward recovered, and
married another girl—a very excellent one she was, too.

Children came to both families. Mary did her honest best
to reform her husband, but the contract was too large. George
went on drinking, and by and by he fell to misusing her and
the little ones sadly. A great many good people strove with
George—they were always at it, in fact—but he calmly took
such efforts as his due and their duty, and did not mend his
ways. He added a vice, presently—that of secret gambling. He
got deeply in debt; he borrowed money on the firm's credit,
as quietly as he could, and carried this system so far and so
successfully that one morning the sheriff took possession of

the establishment, and the two cousins found themselves penniless.

Times were hard, now, and they grew worse. Edward moved his family into a garret, and walked the streets day and night, seeking work. He begged for it, but it was really not to be had. He was astonished to see how soon his face became unwelcome; he was astonished and hurt to see how quickly the ancient interest which people had had in him faded out and disappeared. Still, he *must* get work; so he swallowed his chagrin, and toiled on in search of it. At last he got a job of carrying bricks up a ladder in a hod, and was a grateful man in consequence; but after that *nobody* knew him or cared anything about him. He was not able to keep up his dues in the various moral organizations to which he belonged, and had to endure the sharp pain of seeing himself brought under the disgrace of suspension.

But the faster Edward died out of public knowledge and interest, the faster George rose in them. He was found lying, ragged and drunk, in the gutter one morning. A member of the Ladies' Temperance Refuge fished him out, took him in hand, got up a subscription for him, kept him sober a whole week, then got a situation for him. An account of it was published.

General attention was thus drawn to the poor fellow, and a great many people came forward, and helped him toward reform with their countenance and encouragement. He did not drink a drop for two months, and meantime was the pet of the good. Then he fell—in the gutter; and there was general sorrow and lamentation. But the noble sisterhood rescued him again. They cleaned him up, they fed him, they listened to the mournful music of his repentances, they got him his situation again. An account of this, also, was published, and the town was drowned in happy tears over the re-restoration of the poor beast and struggling victim of the fatal bowl. A grand temperance revival was got up, and after some rousing speeches had been made the chairman said, impressively: "We are now about to call for signers; and I think there is a spectacle in store for you which not many in this house will be able to view with dry eyes." There was an eloquent pause, and then George Benton, escorted by a red-sashed detachment of the Ladies of the Refuge, stepped forward upon the platform and signed the pledge. The air was rent with applause, and everybody cried for joy. Everybody wrung the hand of the new convert when the meeting was over; his salary was enlarged next day; he was the talk of the town, and its hero. An account of it was published.

George Benton fell, regularly, every three months, but was faithfully rescued and wrought with, every time, and good situations were found for him. Finally, he was taken around the country lecturing, as a reformed drunkard, and he had great houses and did an immense amount of good.

He was so popular at home, and so trusted—during his sober intervals—that he was enabled to use the name of a principal citizen, and get a large sum of money at the bank.

A mighty pressure was brought to bear to save him from the consequences of his forgery, and it was partially successful— he was "sent up" for only two years. When, at the end of a year, the tireless efforts of the benevolent were crowned with success, and he emerged from the penitentiary with a pardon in his pocket, the Prisoner's Friend Society met him at the door with a situation and a comfortable salary, and all the other benevolent people came forward and gave him advice, encouragement, and help. Edward Mills had once applied to the Prisoner's Friend Society for a situation, when in dire need, but the question, "Have you been a prisoner?" made brief work of his case.

While all these things were going on, Edward Mills had been quietly making head against adversity. He was still poor, but was in receipt of a steady and sufficient salary, as the respected and trusted cashier of a bank. George Benton never came near him, and was never heard to inquire about him. George got to indulging in long absences from the town; there were ill reports about him, but nothing definite.

One winter's night some masked burglars forced their way into the bank, and found Edward Mills there alone. They commanded him to reveal the "combination," so that they could get into the safe. He refused. They threatened his life. He said his employers trusted him, and he could not be traitor to that trust. He could die, if he must, but while he lived he would be faithful; he would not yield up the "combination." The burglars killed him.

The detectives hunted down the criminals; the chief one proved to be George Benton. A wide sympathy was felt for the widow and orphans of the dead man, and all the newspapers in the land begged that all the banks in the land would testify their appreciation of the fidelity and heroism of the murdered cashier by coming forward with a generous contribution of money in aid of his family, now bereft of support. The result was a mass of solid cash amounting to upward of five hundred dollars—an average of nearly three-eighths of a cent for each bank in the Union. The cashier's own bank testified its gratitude by endeavoring to show (but humiliatingly failed in it) that the peerless servant's accounts were not square, and that he himself had knocked his brains out with a bludgeon to escape detection and punishment.

George Benton was arraigned for trial. Then everybody seemed to forget the widow and orphans in their solicitude for poor George. Everything that money and influence could do was done to save him, but it all failed; he was sentenced to death. Straightway the governor was besieged with petitions for commutation or pardon; they were brought by tearful young girls; by sorrowful old maids; by deputations of pathetic widows; by shoals of impressive orphans. But no, the governor—for once—would not yield.

Now George Benton experienced religion. The glad news flew all around. From that time forth his cell was always full of girls and women and fresh flowers; all the day long there was prayer, and hymn-singing, and thanksgivings, and homilies, and tears, with never an interruption, except an occasional five-minute intermission for refreshments.

This sort of thing continued up to the very gallows, and George Benton went proudly home, in the black cap, before a wailing audience of the sweetest and best that the region could produce. His grave had fresh flowers on it every day, for a while, and the head-stone bore these words, under a hand pointing aloft: "He has fought the good fight."

The brave cashier's head-stone has this inscription:

> Be pure, honest, sober, industrious,
> considerate, and you will never—

Nobody knows who gave the order to leave it that way, but it was so given.

The cashier's family are in stringent circumstances, now, it is said; but no matter; a lot of appreciative people, who were not willing that an act so brave and true as his should go unrewarded, have collected forty-two thousand dollars—and built a Memorial Church with it.

*(Originally published under the same title
in the* Atlantic Monthly, *August 1880)*

Stretching the Truth

When in doubt, tell the truth.

Truth is the most valuable thing we have.
Let us economize it.

A Wellspring of Truth

Throughout his life, Mark Twain explored the fine line separating truth from lies.

I am used to having my statements discounted. My mother had begun it before I was seven years old. But all through my life my facts have had a substratum of truth, and therefore they were not without value. Any person who is familiar with me knows how to strike my average, and therefore knows how to get at the jewel of any fact of mine and dig it out of its blue-clay matrix. My mother knew that art. When I was seven or eight or ten or twelve years old—along there—a neighbor said to her,

"Do you ever believe anything that that boy says?"

My mother said, "He is the wellspring of truth, but you can't bring up the whole well with one bucket"—and she added, "I know his average, therefore he never deceives me. I discount him thirty per cent for embroidery, and what is left is perfect and priceless truth, without a flaw in it anywhere."

(from his autobiography)

George Washington's Inability to Lie

In a sketch written on the occasion of George Washington's birthday, Mark Twain considers how vastly overpraised the Father of the Country was for his alleged inability to lie.

This day, many years ago precisely, George Washington was born. How full of significance the thought! Especially to those among us who have had a similar experience, though subsequently; and still more especially to the young, who should take him for a model and faithfully try to be like him, undeterred by the frequency with which the same thing has been attempted by American youths before them and not satisfactorily accomplished. George Washington was the youngest of nine children, eight of whom were the offspring of his uncle and his aunt. As a boy he gave no promise of the greatness he was one day to achieve. He was ignorant of the commonest accomplishments of youth. He could not even lie. But then he never had any of those precious advantages which are within the reach of the humblest of the boys of the present day. Any boy can lie, now. I could lie before I could stand—yet this sort of sprightliness was so common in our family that little notice was taken of it. Young George appears to have had no sagacity whatever. It is related of him that he once chopped down his father's favorite cherry tree, and then didn't know enough to keep dark about it. He came near going to sea, once, as a midshipman; but when his mother represented to him that he must necessarily be absent when he was away from home, and that this must continue to be the case until he got back, the sad truth struck him so forcibly that he ordered his trunk ashore, and quietly but firmly refused to serve in the navy and fight the battles of his king so long as the effect of it would be to discommode his mother. The great rule of his life was, that procrastination was the thief of time, and that we should always do unto others. This is the golden rule. Therefore, he would never discommode his mother. . . .

(from "A New Biography of Washington," first published in the Virginia City Territorial Enterprise, *February 1866)*

Benjamin Franklin's
Pernicious Example to Youth

Like many American children growing up in the early nineteenth century, Mark Twain chafed under the pressure of trying to live up to the example of role models such as Ben Franklin.

The subject of this memoir was of a vicious disposition, and early prostituted his talents to the invention of maxims and aphorisms calculated to inflict suffering upon the rising gen-

eration of all subsequent ages. His simplest acts, also, were
contrived with a view to their being held up for the emula-
tion of boys for ever—boys who might otherwise have been
happy. It was in this spirit that he became the son of a soap-
boiler, and probably for no other reason than that the efforts
of all future boys who tried to be anything might be looked
upon with suspicion unless they were the sons of soap-boil-
ers. With a malevolence which is without parallel in history,
he would work all day, and then sit up nights, and let on to
be studying algebra by the light of a smouldering fire, so that
all other boys might have to do that also, or else have Benjamin Franklin thrown up to them. Not satisfied with these
proceedings, he had a fashion of living wholly on bread and
water, and studying astronomy at meal time—a thing which
has brought affliction to millions of boys since, whose fathers
had read Franklin's pernicious biography.

His maxims were full of animosity towards boys. Nowa-
days a boy cannot follow out a single natural instinct without
tumbling over some of those everlasting aphorisms and hearing from Franklin on the spot. If he buys two cents' worth of
peanuts, his father says, "Remember what Franklin has said,
my son—'A groat a day's a penny a year;'" and the comfort
is all gone out of those peanuts. If he wants to spin his top
when he has done work, his father quotes, "Procrastination
is the thief of time." If he does a virtuous action, he never gets
anything for it, because "Virtue is its own reward." And that

boy is hounded to death and robbed of his natural rest, because Franklin said once, in one of his inspired flights of malignity—

> Early to bed and early to rise
> Makes a man healthy and wealthy
> and wise.

As if it were any object to a boy to be healthy and wealthy and wise on such terms. The sorrow that that maxim has cost me through my parents' experimenting on me with it, tongue cannot tell. The legitimate result is my present state of general debility, indigence, and mental aberration. My parents used to have me up before nine o'clock in the morning, sometimes, when I was a boy. If they had let me take my natural rest, where would I have been now? Keeping store, no doubt, and respected by all. . . .

When I was a child I had to boil soap, notwithstanding my father was wealthy, and I had to get up early and study geometry at breakfast, and peddle my own poetry, and do everything just as Franklin did, in the solemn hope that I would be a Franklin some day. And here I am.

(from "The Late Benjamin Franklin,"
first published in Galaxy, *July 1870)*

Divine Providence

Providence always makes it a point to find out
what you are after, so as to see that you don't get it.

The proverb says that Providence protects children and idiots.
This is really true. I know it because I have tested it.

A Burning Conscience

As a boy Mark Twain witnessed several grisly deaths. On one occasion he gave matches to a drunk just before the man was put in the town's tiny jail. The man then set fire to his cell and was burned to death before anyone could free him, leaving Mark Twain feeling personally responsible.

The calaboose victim was not a citizen; he was a poor stranger, a harmless, whisky-sodden tramp. I know more about his case than anybody else; I knew too much of it, in that bygone day, to relish speaking of it. That tramp was wandering about the streets one chilly evening, with a pipe in his mouth, and begging for a match; he got neither matches nor courtesy; on the contrary, a troop of bad little boys followed him around and amused themselves with nagging and annoying him. I assisted; but at last, some appeal which the wayfarer made for forbearance, accompanying it with a pathetic reference to his forlorn and friendless condition, touched such sense of shame and remnant of right feeling as were left in me, and I went away and got him some matches, and then hied me home and to bed, heavily weighted as to conscience, and unbuoyant in spirit. An hour or two afterward, the man was arrested and locked up in the calaboose by the marshal—large name for a constable, but that was his title. At two in the morning, the church-bells rang for fire, and everybody turned out, of course—I with the rest. The tramp had used his matches disastrously: he had set his straw bed on fire, and the oaken sheathing of the room had caught. When I reached the ground, two hundred men, women, and children stood massed together, transfixed with horror, and staring at the grated windows of the jail. Behind the iron bars, and tugging frantically at them, and screaming for help, stood the tramp; he seemed like a black object set against a sun, so white and intense was the light at his back. That marshal could not be found, and he had the only key. A battering-ram was quickly improvised, and the thunder of its blows upon the door had so encouraging a sound that the spectators broke into wild cheering, and believed the merciful battle won. But it was not so. The timbers were too strong; they did not yield. It was said that the man's death-grip still held fast to the bars after he was dead; and that in this position the fires wrapped him about and consumed him. As to this, I do not know. What was seen after I recognized the face that was pleading through the bars was seen by others, not by me.

I saw that face, so situated, every night for a long time afterward; and I believed myself as guilty of the man's death as if I had given him the matches purposely that he might burn himself up with them. I had not a doubt that I should be hanged if my connection with this tragedy were found out. The happenings and the impressions of that time are burnt into my memory, and the study of them entertains me as much now as they themselves distressed me then. If anybody spoke of that grisly matter, I was all ears in a moment, and alert to hear what might be said, for I was always dreading and expecting to find out that I was suspected; and so fine and so delicate was the perception of my guilty conscience, that it often detected suspicion in the most purposeless remarks, and in looks, gestures, glances of the eye, which had no significance, but which sent me shivering away in a panic of fright, just the same. And how sick it made me when somebody dropped, howsoever carelessly and barren of intent, the remark that "murder will out!" For a boy of ten years, I was carrying a pretty weighty cargo.

All this time I was blessedly forgetting one thing—the fact that I was an inveterate talker in my sleep. But one night I awoke and found my bed-mate—my younger brother—sitting up in bed and contemplating me by the light of the moon. I said:

"What is the matter?"

"You talk so much I can't sleep."

I came to a sitting posture in an instant, with my kidneys in my throat and my hair on end.

"What did I say? Quick—out with it—what did I say?"

"Nothing much."

"It's a lie—you know everything."

"Everything about what?"

"You know well enough. About *that*."

"About *what*? I don't know what you are talking about. I think you are sick or crazy or something. But anyway, you're awake, and I'll get to sleep while I've got a chance."

He fell asleep and I lay there in a cold sweat, turning this new terror over in the whirling chaos which did duty as my mind. The burden of my thought was, How much did I divulge? How much does he know? What a distress is this uncertainty! But by and by I evolved an idea—I would wake my brother and probe him with a supposititious case. I shook him up, and said:

"Suppose a man should come to you drunk—"

"This is foolish—I never get drunk."

"I don't mean you, idiot—I mean the man. Suppose a *man* should come to you drunk, and borrow a knife, or a tomahawk, or a pistol, and you forgot to tell him it was loaded, and—"

"How could you load a tomahawk?"

"I don't mean the tomahawk, and I didn't *say* the tomahawk; I said the pistol. Now don't you keep breaking in that way, because this is serious. There's been a man killed."

"What! In this town?"

"Yes, in this town."

"Well, go on—I won't say a single word."

"Well, then, suppose you forgot to tell him to be careful with it, because it was loaded, and he went off and shot himself with that pistol—fooling with it, you know, and probably doing it by accident, being drunk. Well, would it be murder?"

"No—suicide."

"No, no. I don't mean *his* act, I mean yours. Would you be a murderer for letting him have that pistol?"

After deep thought came this answer:

"Well, I should think I was guilty of something—maybe murder—yes, probably murder, but I don't quite know."

This made me very uncomfortable. However, it was not a decisive verdict. I should have to set out the real case—there seemed to be no other way. But I would do it cautiously, and keep a watch out for suspicious effects. I said:

"I was supposing a case, but I am coming to the real one now. Do you know how the man came to be burned up in the calaboose?"

"No."

"Haven't you the least idea?"

"Not the least."

"Wish you may die in your tracks if you have?"

"Yes, wish I may die in my tracks."

"Well, the way of it was this. The man wanted some matches to light his pipe. A boy got him some. The man set fire to the calaboose with those very matches, and burnt himself up."

"Is that so?"

"Yes, it is. Now, is that boy a murderer, do you think?"

"Let me see. The man was drunk?"

"Yes, he was drunk."

"Very drunk?"

"Yes."

"And the boy knew it?"

"Yes, he knew it."

There was a long pause. Then came this heavy verdict:

"If the man was drunk, and the boy knew it, the boy murdered that man. This is certain."

Faint, sickening sensations crept along all the fibers of my body, and I seemed to know how a person feels who hears his death-sentence pronounced from the bench. I waited to hear what my brother would say next. I believed I knew what it would be, and I was right. He said:

"I know the boy."

I had nothing to say; so I said nothing. I simply shuddered. Then he added:

"Yes, before you got half through telling about the thing, I knew perfectly well who the boy was; it was Ben Coontz!"

I came out of my collapse as one who rises from the dead. I said, with admiration:

"Why, how in the world did you ever guess it?"

"You told me in your sleep."

I said to myself, "How splendid that is! This is a habit which must be cultivated."

My brother rattled innocently on:

"When you were talking in your sleep, you kept mumbling something about 'matches,' which I couldn't make anything out of; but just now, when you began to tell me about the man and the calaboose and the matches, I remembered that in your sleep you mentioned Ben Coontz two or three times; so I put this and that together, you see, and right away I knew it was Ben that burnt that man up."

I praised his sagacity effusively. Presently he asked:

"Are you going to give him up to the law?"

"No," I said, "I believe that this will be a lesson to him. I shall keep an eye on him, of course, for that is but right; but if he stops where he is and reforms, it shall never be said that I betrayed him."

"How good you are!"

"Well, I try to be. It is all a person can do in a world like this."

And now, my burden being shifted to other shoulders, my terrors soon faded away.

The day before we left Hannibal, a curious thing fell under my notice—the surprising spread which longitudinal time undergoes there. I learned it from one of the most unostentatious of men—the colored coachman of a friend of mine, who lives three miles from town. He was to call for me at the Park Hotel at 7.30 P.M., and drive me out. But he missed it considerably—did not arrive till ten. He excused himself by saying:

"De time is mos' an hour en a half slower in de country en what it is in de town; you'll be in plenty time, boss. Sometimes we shoves out early for church, Sunday, en fetches up dah right plum in de middle er de sermon. Diffunce in de time. A body can't make no calculations 'bout it."

I had lost two hours and a half; but I had learned a fact worth four.

(from Life on the Mississippi, *1883, chapter 56)*

A Boy's Life Is Not All Comedy

The incident of the drunk burning to death was one of several grisly deaths that Mark Twain witnessed as a boy. Many of these incidents—which weighed on his conscience—he later used in his fiction.

*B*ut a boy's life is not all comedy; much of the tragic enters into it. The drunken tramp—mentioned elsewhere—who was burned up in the village jail lay upon my conscience a hundred nights afterward and filled them with hideous dreams— dreams in which I saw his appealing face as I had seen it in the pathetic reality, pressed against the window bars, with the red hell glowing behind him—a face which seemed to say to me, "If you had not given me the matches, this would not have happened; you are responsible for my death." I was *not* responsible for it, for I had meant him no harm, but only good, when I let him have the matches; but no matter, mine was a trained Presbyterian conscience and knew but the one duty— to hunt and harry its slave upon all pretexts and on all occasions, particularly when there was no sense nor reason in it. The tramp—who was to blame—suffered ten minutes; I, who was not to blame, suffered three months.

The shooting down of poor old Smarr in the main street at noonday supplied me with some more dreams; and in them I always saw again the grotesque closing picture—the great family Bible spread open on the profane old man's breast by some thoughtful idiot, and rising and sinking to the labored breathings, and adding the torture of its leaden weight to the dying struggles. We are curiously made. In all the throng of gaping and sympathetic onlookers there was not one with common sense enough to perceive that an anvil would have been in better taste there than the Bible, less open to sarcastic criticism, and swifter in its atrocious work. In my nightmares I gasped and struggled for breath under the crush of that vast book for many a night.

All within the space of a couple of years we had two or three other tragedies, and I had the ill luck to be too near by, on each occasion. There was the slave man who was struck down with a chunk of slag for some small offense; I saw him die. And the young Californian emigrant who was stabbed with a bowie knife by a drunken comrade; I saw the red life gush from his breast. And the case of the rowdy young brothers and their harmless old uncle: one of them held the old man down with his knees on his breast while the other one tried repeatedly to kill him with an Allen revolver which wouldn't go off. I happened along just then, of course.

Then there was the case of the young Californian emigrant who got drunk and proposed to raid the "Welshman's house" all alone one dark and threatening night. This house stood halfway up Holliday's Hill and its sole occupants were a poor but quite respectable widow and her blameless daughter. The invading ruffian woke the whole village with his ribald yells and coarse challenges and obscenities. I went up there with a comrade—John Briggs, I think—to look and listen. The figure of the man was dimly visible; the women were on their porch, not visible in the deep shadow of its roof, but we heard the elder woman's voice. She had loaded an old musket with slugs, and she warned the man that if he stayed where he was while she counted ten it would cost him his life. She began to count, slowly; he began to laugh. He stopped laughing at "six"; then through the deep stillness, in a steady voice, followed the rest of the tale: "Seven . . . eight . . . nine"—a long pause, we holding our breaths—"ten!" A red spout of flame gushed out into the night, and the man dropped with his breast riddled to rags. Then the rain and the thunder burst loose and the waiting town swarmed up the hill in the glare of the lightning like an invasion of ants. Those people saw the rest; I had had my share and was satisfied. I went home to dream, and was not disappointed.

My teaching and training enabled me to see deeper into these tragedies than an ignorant person could have done. I knew what they were for. I tried to disguise it from myself, but down in the secret deeps of my troubled heart I knew—and I *knew* I knew. They were inventions of Providence to beguile me to a better life. It sounds curiously innocent and conceited, now, but to me there was nothing strange about it; it was quite in accordance with the thoughtful and judicious ways of Providence as I understood them. It would not have surprised me, nor even overflattered me, if Providence had killed off that whole community in trying to save an asset like me. Educated as I had been, it would have seemed just the thing, and well worth the expense. *Why* Providence should take such an anxious interest in such a property, that idea never entered my head, and there was no one in that simple hamlet who would have dreamed of putting it there. For one thing, no one was equipped with it.

It is quite true, I took all the tragedies to myself, and tallied them off in turn as they happened, saying to myself in each case, with a sigh, "Another one gone—and on my account; this ought to bring me to repentance; the patience of God will not always endure." And yet privately I believed it would. That is, I believed it in the daytime; but not in the night. With the going down of the sun my faith failed and the clammy fears gathered about my heart. It was then that I repented. Those were awful nights, nights of despair, nights charged with the bitterness of death. After each tragedy I recognized the warning and repented; repented and begged; begged like a coward, begged like a dog; and not in the interest of those poor people who had been extinguished for my sake, but only in my *own* interest. It seems selfish, when I look back on it now.

My repentances were very real, very earnest; and after each tragedy they happened every night for a long time. But as a rule they could not stand the daylight. They faded out and shredded away and disappeared in the glad splendor of the sun. They were the creatures of fear and darkness, and they could not live out of their own place. The day gave me cheer and peace, and at night I repented again. In all my boyhood life I am not sure that I ever tried to lead a better life in the daytime—or wanted to. In my age I should never think of wishing to do such a thing. But in my age, as in my youth, night brings me many a deep remorse. I realize that from the cradle up I have been like the rest of the race—never quite sane in the night. When "Injun Joe" died . . . But never mind. Somewhere I have already described what a raging hell of repentance I passed through then. I believe that for months I was as pure as the driven snow. After dark.

(from his autobiography)

The Drownings of
Lem Hackett and Dutchy

During Mark Twain's return to Hannibal in 1882, he walked among the aging houses and recalled neighbors whom he had once known and the strange manner in which Providence had treated two of his boyhood friends.

Among them I presently recognized the house of the father of Lem Hackett (fictitious name). It carried me back more than a generation in a moment, and landed me in the midst of a time when the happenings of life were not the natural and logical results of great general laws, but of special orders, and

were freighted with very precise and distinct purposes—partly
punitive in intent, partly admonitory; and usually local in
application.

When I was a small boy, Lem Hackett was drowned—on
a Sunday. He fell out of an empty flat-boat, where he was
playing. Being loaded with sin, he went to the bottom like an
anvil. He was the only boy in the village who slept that night.
We others all lay awake, repenting. We had not needed the
information, delivered from the pulpit that evening, that Lem's
was a case of special judgment—we knew that, already. There
was a ferocious thunder-storm that night, and it raged con-
tinuously until near dawn. The wind blew, the windows rattled, the rain swept along the roof in pelting sheets, and at
the briefest of intervals the inky blackness of the night van-
ished, the houses over the way glared out white and blinding
for a quivering instant, then the solid darkness shut down
again and a splitting peal of thunder followed which seemed
to rend everything in the neighborhood to shreds and splin-
ters. I sat up in bed quaking and shuddering, waiting for the
destruction of the world, and expecting it. To me there was
nothing strange or incongruous in Heaven's making such an
uproar about Lem Hackett. Apparently it was the right and
proper thing to do. Not a doubt entered my mind that all the
angels were grouped together, discussing this boy's case and
observing the awful bombardment of our beggarly little village with satisfaction and approval. There was one thing
which disturbed me in the most serious way; that was the

thought that this centering of the celestial interest on our village could not fail to attract the attention of the observers to
people among us who might otherwise have escaped notice
for years. I felt that I was not only one of those people, but
the very one most likely to be discovered. That discovery
could have but one result: I should be in the fire with Lem
before the chill of the river had been fairly warmed out of him.
I knew that this would be only just and fair. I was increasing
the chances against myself all the time, by feeling a secret bitterness against Lem for having attracted this fatal attention to
me, but I could not help it—this sinful thought persisted in
infesting my breast in spite of me. Every time the lightning
glared I caught my breath, and judged I was gone. In my terror and misery, I meanly began to suggest other boys, and
mention acts of theirs which were wickeder than mine, and
peculiarly needed punishment—and I tried to pretend to
myself that I was simply doing this in a casual way, and without intent to divert the heavenly attention to them for the purpose of getting rid of it myself. With deep sagacity I put these
mentions into the form of sorrowing recollections and left-
handed sham-supplications that the sins of those boys might
be allowed to pass unnoticed—"Possibly they may repent." "It
is true that Jim Smith broke a window and lied about it—but
maybe he did not mean any harm. And although Tom Holmes
says more bad words than any other boy in the village, he
probably intends to repent—though he has never said he
would. And whilst it is a fact that John Jones did fish a little

on Sunday, once, he didn't really catch anything but only just one small useless mud-cat; and maybe that wouldn't have been so awful if he had thrown it back—as he says he did, but he didn't. Pity but they would repent of these dreadful things—and maybe they will yet."

But while I was shamefully trying to draw attention to these poor chaps—who were doubtless directing the celestial attention to me at the same moment, though I never once suspected that—I had heedlessly left my candle burning. It was not a time to neglect even trifling precautions. There was no occasion to add anything to the facilities for attracting notice to me—so I put the light out.

It was a long night to me, and perhaps the most distressful one I ever spent. I endured agonies of remorse for sins which I knew I had committed, and for others which I was not certain about, yet was sure that they had been set down against me in a book by an angel who was wiser than I and did not trust such important matters to memory. It struck me, by and by, that I had been making a most foolish and calamitous mistake, in one respect; doubtless I had not only made my own destruction sure by directing attention to those other boys, but had already accomplished theirs! Doubtless the lightning had stretched them all dead in their beds by this time! The anguish and the fright which this thought gave me made my previous sufferings seem trifling by comparison.

Things had become truly serious. I resolved to turn over a new leaf instantly; I also resolved to connect myself with the church the next day, if I survived to see its sun appear. I resolved to cease from sin in all its forms, and to lead a high and blameless life forever after. I would be punctual at church and Sunday-school; visit the sick; carry baskets of victuals to the poor (simply to fulfil the regulation conditions, although I knew we had none among us so poor but they would smash the basket over my head for my pains); I would instruct other boys in right ways, and take the resulting trouncings meekly; I would subsist entirely on tracts; I would invade the rum shop and warn the drunkard—and finally, if I escaped the fate of those who early become too good to live, I would go for a missionary.

The storm subsided toward daybreak, and I dozed gradually to sleep with a sense of obligation to Lem Hackett for going to eternal suffering in that abrupt way, and thus preventing a far more dreadful disaster—my own loss.

But when I rose refreshed, by and by, and found that those other boys were still alive, I had a dim sense that perhaps the whole thing was a false alarm; that the entire turmoil had been on Lem's account and nobody's else. The world looked so bright and safe that there did not seem to be any real occasion to turn over a new leaf. I was a little subdued, during that day, and perhaps the next; after that, my purpose of reforming slowly dropped out of my mind, and I had a peaceful, comfortable time again, until the next storm.

That storm came about three weeks later; and it was the most unaccountable one, to me, that I had ever experienced;

for on the afternoon of that day, "Dutchy" was drowned. Dutchy belonged to our Sunday-school. He was a German lad who did not know enough to come in out of the rain; but he was exasperatingly good, and had a prodigious memory. One Sunday he made himself the envy of all the youth and the talk of all the admiring village, by reciting three thousand verses of Scripture without missing a word; then he went off the very next day and got drowned.

Circumstances gave to his death a peculiar impressiveness. We were all bathing in a muddy creek which had a deep hole in it, and in this hole the coopers had sunk a pile of green hickory hoop-poles to soak, some twelve feet under water. We were diving and "seeing who could stay under longest." We managed to remain down by holding on to the hoop-poles. Dutchy made such a poor success of it that he was hailed with laughter and derision every time his head appeared above water. At last he seemed hurt with the taunts, and begged us to stand still on the bank and be fair with him and give him an honest count—"be friendly and kind just this once, and not miscount for the sake of having the fun of laughing at him." Treacherous winks were exchanged, and all said "All right, Dutchy—go ahead, we'll play fair."

Dutchy plunged in, but the boys, instead of beginning to count, followed the lead of one of their number and scampered to a range of blackberry bushes close by and hid behind it. They imagined Dutchy's humiliation, when he should rise after a superhuman effort and find the place silent and vacant, nobody there to applaud. They were "so full of laugh" with the idea that they were continually exploding into muffled cackles. Time swept on, and presently one who was peeping through the briers, said, with surprise:

"Why, he hasn't come up yet!"

The laughing stopped.

"Boys, it's a splendid dive," said one.

"Never mind that," said another, "the joke on him is all the better for it."

There was a remark or two more, and then a pause. Talking ceased, and all began to peer through the vines. Before long, the boys' faces began to look uneasy, then anxious, then terrified. Still there was no movement of the placid water. Hearts began to beat fast, and faces to turn pale. We all glided out, silently, and stood on the bank, our horrified eyes wandering back and forth from each other's countenances to the water.

"Somebody must go down and see!"

Yes, that was plain; but nobody wanted that grisly task.

"Draw straws!"

So we did—with hands which shook so, that we hardly knew what we were about. The lot fell to me, and I went down. The water was so muddy I could not see anything, but I felt around among the hoop-poles, and presently grasped a limp wrist which gave me no response—and if it had I should not have known it, I let it go with such a frightened suddenness.

The boy had been caught among the hoop-poles and entangled there, helplessly. I fled to the surface and told the awful news. Some of us knew that if the boy were dragged out at once he might possibly be resuscitated, but we never thought of that. We did not think of anything; we did not know what to do, so we did nothing—except that the smaller lads cried piteously, and we all struggled frantically into our clothes, putting on anybody's that came handy, and getting them wrong-side-out and upside-down, as a rule. Then we scurried away and gave the alarm, but none of us went back to see the end of the tragedy. We had a more important thing to attend to: we all flew home, and lost not a moment in getting ready to lead a better life.

The night presently closed down. Then came on that tremendous and utterly unaccountable storm. I was perfectly dazed; I could not understand it. It seemed to me that there must be some mistake. The elements were turned loose, and they rattled and banged and blazed away in the most blind and frantic manner. All heart and hope went out of me, and the dismal thought kept floating through my brain, "If a boy who knows three thousand verses by heart is not satisfactory, what chance is there for anybody else?"

Of course I never questioned for a moment that the storm was on Dutchy's account, or that he or any other inconsequential animal was worthy of such a majestic demonstration from on high; the lesson of it was the only thing that troubled me; for it convinced me that if Dutchy, with all his perfections, was not a delight, it would be vain for me to turn over a new leaf, for I must infallibly fall hopelessly short of that boy, no matter how hard I might try. Nevertheless I did turn it over—a highly educated fear compelled me to do that—but succeeding days of cheerfulness and sunshine came bothering around, and within a month I had so drifted backward that again I was as lost and comfortable as ever.

(from Life on the Mississippi, *1883, chapter 54)*

How to
Get to
Heaven

*When I reflect upon the number of disagreeable
people who I know have gone to a better world,
I am moved to lead a different life.*

*It is not best to use our morals weekdays,
it gets them out of repair for Sunday.*

Ask and Ye Shall Receive

Inclined to interpret Bible texts literally when he was a child,
Mark Twain often had trouble reconciling faith with reality.
Here he recalls his youthful experiments with prayer when he
was Mrs. Horr's young pupil. Huck undergoes a similar
disillusionment in Adventures of Huckleberry Finn.

*M*rs. Horr was a New England lady of middle age with New England ways and principles, and she always opened school with prayer and a chapter from the New Testament; also she explained the chapter with a brief talk. In one of these talks she dwelt upon the text, "Ask and ye shall receive," and said that whosoever prayed for a thing with earnestness and strong desire need not doubt that his prayer would be answered.

I was so forcibly struck by this information and so gratified by the opportunities which it offered that this was probably the first time I had heard of it. I thought I would give it a trial. I believed in Mrs. Horr thoroughly and I had no doubts as to the result. I prayed for gingerbread. Margaret Kooneman, who was the baker's daughter, brought a slab of gingerbread to school every morning; she had always kept it out of sight before but when I finished my prayer and glanced up, there it was in easy reach and she was looking the other way. In all my life I believe I never enjoyed an answer to prayer more than I enjoyed that one; and I was a convert, too. I had no end of wants and they had always remained unsatisfied up to that time, but I meant to supply them and extend them now that I had found out how to do it.

But this dream was like almost all the other dreams we indulge in life, there was nothing in it. I did as much praying during the next two or three days as any one in that town, I suppose, and I was very sincere and earnest about it too, but nothing came of it. I found that not even the powerful prayer was competent to lift that gingerbread again, and I came to the conclusion that if a person remains faithful to his gingerbread and keeps his eye on it, he need not trouble himself about your prayers.

Something about my conduct and bearing troubled my mother, and she took me aside and questioned me concerning it with much solicitude. I was reluctant to reveal to her that change that had come over me, for it would grieve me to distress her kind heart, but at last I confessed, with many tears, that I had ceased to be a Christian. She was heartbroken, and asked me why.

I said it was because I had found out that I was a Christian for revenue only and I could not bear the thought of that, it was so ignoble.

She gathered me to her breast and comforted me. I gathered from what she said that if I would continue in that condition I would never be lonesome.

(from his autobiography)

Tickets to Heaven

*Mark Twain fondly recalled his Methodist Sunday-school
teacher, a stone mason name Richmond, who helped introduce
him to "good boy" literature.*

*H*e was a very kindly and considerate Sunday-school teacher,
and patient and compassionate, so he was the favorite teacher
with us little chaps. In that school they had slender oblong
pasteboard blue tickets, each with a verse from the Testament
printed on it, and you could get a blue ticket by reciting two
verses. By reciting five verses you could get three blue tickets, and you could trade these at the bookcase and borrow a
book for a week. I was under Mr. Richmond's spiritual care
every now and then for two or three years, and he was never
hard upon me. I always recited the same five verses every
Sunday. He was always satisfied with the performance. He
never seemed to notice that these were the same five foolish
virgins that he had been hearing about every Sunday for
months. I always got my tickets and exchanged them for a
book. They were pretty dreary books, for there was not a bad
boy in the entire bookcase. They were all good boys and good
girls and drearily uninteresting, but they were better society
than none, and I was glad to have their company and disap-
prove of it.

(from his autobiography)

Squaring Crimes by Going to Church

As a boy, Mark Twain was occasionally ordered to attend extra church services as a punishment. Sometimes his failure to get to church led to additional punishments.

*W*henever my conduct was of such exaggerated impropriety that my mother's extemporary punishments were inadequate, she saved the matter up for Sunday and made me go to church Sunday night—which was a penalty sometimes bearable, perhaps, but as a rule it was not, and I avoided it for the sake of my constitution. She would never believe that I had been to church until she had applied her test. She made me tell her what the text was. That was a simple matter—caused me no trouble. I didn't have to go to church to get a text. I selected one for myself. This worked very well until one time when my text and the one furnished by a neighbor, who had been to church, didn't tally. After that my mother took other methods. I don't know what they were now.

In those days men and boys wore rather long cloaks in the wintertime. They were black, and were lined with very bright and showy Scotch plaids. One winter's night when I was starting to church to square a crime of some kind committed during the week, I hid my cloak near the gate and went off and played with the other boys until church was over. Then I returned home. But in the dark I put the cloak on wrong side out, entered the room, threw the cloak aside, and then stood the usual examination. I got along very well until the temperature of the church was mentioned. My mother said, "It must have been impossible to keep warm there on such a night."

I didn't see the art of that remark, and was foolish enough to explain that I wore my cloak all the time that I was in church. She asked if I kept it on from church home, too. I didn't see the bearing of that remark. I said that that was what I had done. She said: "You wore it with that red Scotch plaid outside and glaring? Didn't that attract any attention?"

Of course to continue such a dialogue would have been tedious and unprofitable, and I let it go and took the consequences.

(from his autobiography)

How to Behave at a Funeral

Although often irreverent, Mark Twain believed strongly in showing proper respect for the dead.

Do not criticize the person in whose honor the entertainment is given.

Make no remarks about his equipment. If the handles are plated, it is best to seem to not observe it.

If the odor of the flowers is too oppressive for your comfort, remember that they were not brought there for you, and

that the person for whom they were brought suffers no incon-
venience from their presence.

Listen, with as intense an expression of attention as you
can command, to the official statement of the character and
history of the person in whose honor the entertainment is
given; and if these statistics should seem to fail to tally with
the facts, in places, do not nudge your neighbor, or press your
foot upon his toes, or manifest, by any other sign, your aware-
ness that taffy is being distributed.

If the official hopes expressed concerning the person in
whose honor the entertainment is given are known by you to
be oversized, let it pass—do not interrupt.

At the moving passages, be moved—but only according to
the degree of your intimacy with the parties giving the entertainment, or with the party in whose honor the entertainment
is given. Where a blood relation sobs, an intimate friend
should choke up, a distant relation should sigh, a stranger
should merely fumble sympathetically with his handkerchief.
Where the occasion is military, the emotions should be graded
according to military rank, the highest officer present taking
precedence in emotional violence, and the rest modifying their
feelings according to their position in the service.

Do not bring your dog.

(from an unfinished burlesque on etiquette, c. 1881)

Cheating Death

Each person is born to one possession
which outvalues all his others—his last breath.

We can't reach old age by another man's road.
My habits protect my life but they would assassinate you.

A Sickly Child

I was always told that I was a sickly and precarious and tiresome and uncertain child, and lived mainly on allopathic medicines during the first seven years of my life. I asked my mother about this, in her old age—she was in her eighty-eighth year—and said:

"I suppose that during all that time you were uneasy about me?"

"Yes, the whole time."

"Afraid I wouldn't live?"

After a reflective pause—ostensibly to think out the facts—"No—afraid you would."

(from his autobiography)

Tom Sawyer Shares His
Medicine with a Cat

*Mark Twain modeled Tom Sawyer's Aunt Polly on his own
mother, an ardent believer in patent medicines and quack
cures. Once his mother so overdosed him that he tried to share
the burden with the family cat.* The Adventures of Tom
Sawyer *re-creates this incident, when Aunt Polly tries to
relieve Tom's melancholy with patent medicines.*

She began to try all manner of remedies on him. She was one
of those people who are infatuated with patent medicines and
all new-fangled methods of producing health or mending it.
She was an inveterate experimenter in these things. When
something fresh in this line came out she was in a fever, right
away, to try it; not on herself, for she was never ailing, but on
anybody else that came handy. She was a subscriber for all
the "Health" periodicals and phreneological frauds; and the
solemn ignorance they were inflated with was breath to her
nostrils. All the "rot" they contained about ventilation, and
how to go to bed, and how to get up, and what to eat, and
what to drink, and how much exercise to take, and what frame
of mind to keep one's self in, and what sort of clothing to
wear, was all gospel to her, and she never observed that her
health-journals of the current month customarily upset everything they had recommended the month before. She was as
simple-hearted and honest as the day was long, and so she was

an easy victim. She gathered together her quack periodicals and her quack medicines, and thus armed with death, went about on her pale horse, metaphorically speaking, with "hell following after." But she never suspected that she was not an angel of healing and the balm of Gilead in disguise, to the suffering neighbors.

The water treatment was new, now, and Tom's low condition was a windfall to her. She had him out at daylight every morning, stood him up in the woodshed and drowned him with a deluge of cold water; then she scrubbed him down with a towel like a file, and so brought him to; then she rolled him up in a wet sheet and put him away under blankets till she sweated his soul clean and "the yellow stains of it came through his pores"—as Tom said.

Yet notwithstanding all this, the boy grew more and more melancholy and pale and dejected. She added hot baths, sitz baths, shower baths and plunges. The boy remained as dismal as a hearse. She began to assist the water with a slim oatmeal diet and blister plasters. She calculated his capacity as she would a jug's, and filled him up every day with quack cure-alls.

Tom had become indifferent to persecution by this time. This phase filled the old lady's heart with consternation. This indifference must be broken up at any cost. Now she heard of Pain-killer for the first time. She ordered a lot at once. She tasted it and was filled with gratitude. It was simply fire in a liquid form. She dropped the water treatment and everything else, and pinned her faith to Pain-killer. She gave Tom a teaspoonful and watched with the deepest anxiety for the result. Her troubles were instantly at rest, her soul at peace again; for the "indifference" was broken up. The boy could not have shown a wilder, heartier interest, if she had built a fire under him.

Tom felt that it was time to wake up; this sort of life might be romantic enough, in his blighted condition, but it was getting to have too little sentiment and too much distracting variety about it. So he thought over various plans for relief, and finally hit upon that of professing to be fond of Pain-killer. He asked for it so often that he became a nuisance, and his aunt ended by telling him to help himself and quit bothering her. If it had been Sid, she would have had no misgivings to alloy her delight; but since it was Tom, she watched the bottle clandestinely. She found that the medicine did really diminish, but it did not occur to her that the boy was mending the health of a crack in the sitting-room floor with it.

One day Tom was in the act of dosing the crack when his yellow cat came along, purring, eyeing the teaspoon avariciously, and begging for a taste. Tom said:

"Don't ask for it unless you want it, Peter."

But Peter signified that he did want it.

"You better make sure."

Peter was sure.

"Now you've asked for it, and I'll give it to you, because there ain't anything mean about *me*; but if you find you don't like it, you musn't blame anybody but your own self."

Peter was agreeable. So Tom pried his mouth open and poured down the Pain-killer. Peter sprang a couple of yards into the air, and then delivered a war-whoop and set off round and round the room, banging against furniture, upsetting flower pots and making general havoc. Next he rose on his hind feet and pranced around, in a frenzy of enjoyment, with his head over his shoulder and his voice proclaiming his unappeasable happiness. Then he went tearing around the house again spreading chaos and destruction in his path. Aunt Polly entered in time to see him throw a few double summersets, deliver a final mighty hurrah, and sail through the open window, carrying the rest of the flower-pots with him. The old lady stood petrified with astonishment, peering over her glasses; Tom lay on the floor expiring with laughter.

"Tom, what on earth ails that cat?"

"*I* don't know, aunt," gasped the boy.

"Why I never see anything like it. What *did* make him act so?"

"Deed I don't know Aunt Polly; cats always act so when they're having a good time."

"They do, do they?" There was something in the tone that made Tom apprehensive.

"Yes'm. That is, I believe they do."

"You *do*?"

"Yes'm."

The old lady was bending down, Tom watching, with interest emphasized by anxiety. Too late he divined her "drift." The handle of the tell-tale tea-spoon was visible under the bed-valance. Aunt Polly took it, held it up. Tom winced, and dropped his eyes. Aunt Polly raised him by the usual handle— his ear—and cracked his head soundly with her thimble.

"Now, sir, what did you want to treat that poor dumb beast so, for?"

"I done it out of pity for him—because he hadn't any aunt."

"Hadn't any aunt!—you numscull. What has that got to do with it?"

"Heaps. Because if he'd a had one she'd a burnt him out herself! She'd a roasted his bowels out of him 'thout any more feeling than if he was a human!"

Aunt Polly felt a sudden pang of remorse. This was putting the thing in a new light; what was cruelty to a cat *might* be cruelty to a boy, too. She began to soften; she felt sorry. Her eyes watered a little, and she put her hand on Tom's head and said gently:

"I was meaning for the best, Tom. And Tom, it *did* do you good."

Tom looked up in her face with just a perceptible twinkle peeping through his gravity:

"I know you was meaning for the best, aunty, and so was I with Peter. It done *him* good, too. I never see him get around so since—"

(from The Adventures of Tom Sawyer, *1876, chapter 12)*

A Shade of Death's Door

*When a measles epidemic swept Hannibal during Mark
Twain's youth, the fear of catching the disease seemed so much
worse to him than that of actually dying from it that he
decided not to wait for the disease to find him.*

*I*n 1845, when I was ten years old, there was an epidemic of
measles in the town and it made a most alarming slaughter
among the little people. There was a funeral almost daily, and
the mothers of the town were nearly demented with fright. My
mother was greatly troubled. She worried over Pamela and
Henry and me, and took constant and extraordinary pains to
keep us from coming into contact with the contagion. But
upon reflection I believed that her judgment was at fault. It
seemed to me that I could improve upon it if left to my own
devices. I cannot remember now whether I was frightened
about the measles or not, but I clearly remember that I grew
very tired of the suspense I suffered on account of being continually under the threat of death. I remember that I got so
weary of it and so anxious to have the matter settled one way
or the other, and promptly, that this anxiety spoiled my days
and my nights. I had no pleasure in them. I made up my mind
to end this suspense and settle this matter one way or the
other and be done with it. Will Bowen was dangerously ill
with the measles and I thought I would go down there and
catch them. I entered the house by the front way and slipped

along through rooms and halls, keeping sharp watch against discovery, and at last I reached Will's bed-chamber in the rear of the house on the second floor and got into it uncaptured. But that was as far as my victory reached. His mother caught me there a moment later and snatched me out of the house and gave me a most competent scolding and drove me away. She was so scared that she could hardly get her words out, and her face was white. I saw that I must manage better next time, and I did. I hung about the lane at the rear of the house and watched through cracks in the fence until I was convinced that the conditions were favorable; then I slipped through the back yard and up the back way and got into the room and into the bed with Will Bowen without being observed. I don't know how long I was in the bed. I only remember that Will Bowen, as society, had no value for me, for he was too sick to even notice that I was there. When I heard his mother coming I covered up my head, but that device was a failure. It was dead summertime—the cover was nothing more than a limp blanket or sheet, and anybody could see that there were two of us under it. It didn't remain two very long. Mrs. Bowen snatched me out of that bed and conducted me home herself, with a grip on my collar which she never loosened until she delivered me into my mother's hands along with her opinion of that kind of a boy.

It was a good case of measles that resulted. It brought me within a shade of death's door. It brought me to where I no longer felt any interest in anything, but, on the contrary, felt a total absence of interest—which was most placid and tranquil and sweet and delightful and enchanting. I have never enjoyed anything in my life any more than I enjoyed dying that time. I *was*, in effect, dying. The word had been passed and the family notified to assemble around the bed and see me off. I knew them all. There was no doubtfulness in my vision. They were all crying, but that did not affect me. I took but the vaguest interest in it, and that merely because I was the centre of all this emotional attention and was gratified by it and felt complimented.

When Doctor Cunningham had made up his mind that nothing more could be done for me he put bags of hot ashes all over me. He put them on my breast, on my wrists, on my ankles; and so, very much to his astonishment—and doubtless to my regret—he dragged me back into this world and set me going again.

(from his autobiography)

Habits, Good and Bad

Habit is habit, and not to be flung out of the window by any man, but coaxed down-stairs a step at a time.

*Let us swear while we may,
for in heaven it will not be allowed.*

A Grandmother's Influence

In 1870, after Mark Twain read an obituary in which the deceased man credited all his praiseworthy habits to his mother, he recalled the similar (but imaginary) influence that his grandmother had had on him.

*H*ow touching is this tribute of the late Hon. T. H. Benton to his mother's influence:—"My mother asked me never to use tobacco; I have never touched it from that time to the present day. She asked me not to gamble, and I have never gambled. I cannot tell who is losing in games that are being played. She admonished me, too, against liquor-drinking, and whatever capacity for endurance I have at present, and whatever usefulness I may have attained through life, I attribute to having complied with her pious and correct wishes. When I was seven years of age she asked me not to drink, and then I made a resolution of total abstinence; and that I have adhered to it through all time I owe to my mother."

I never saw anything so curious. It is almost an exact epitome of my own moral career—after simply substituting a grandmother for a mother. How well I remember my grandmother's asking me not to use tobacco, good old soul! She said, "You're at it again, are you, you whelp? Now, don't ever let me catch you chewing tobacco before breakfast again, or I lay I'll blacksnake you within an inch of your life!" I have never touched it at that hour of the morning from that time to the present day.

She asked me not to gamble. She whispered and said, "Put up those wicked cards this minute!—two pair and a jack, you numskull, and the other fellow's got a flush!"

I never have gambled from that day to this—never once— without a "cold deck" in my pocket. I cannot even tell who is going to lose in games that are being played unless I dealt myself.

When I was two years of age she asked me not to drink, and then I made a resolution of total abstinence. That I have adhered to it and enjoyed the beneficent effects of it through all time, I owe to my grandmother. I have never drunk a drop from that day to this of any kind of water.

(First published as "History Repeats Itself,"
in Galaxy, *December 1870)*

Learning How to Smoke

*Mark Twain's autobiography recalls how he was pressured
into taking up tobacco-chewing as a young boy, only to make
himself sick. The experience resembles the moment when Huck
Finn teaches Tom Sawyer and Joe Harper how to smoke
during their pirate adventure on a Mississippi River island
in* The Adventures of Tom Sawyer.

*A*fter a dainty egg and fish dinner, Tom said he wanted to
learn to smoke, now. Joe caught at the idea and said he would
like to try, too. So Huck made pipes and filled them. These
novices had never smoked anything before but cigars made
of grape-vine, and they "bit" the tongue and were not considered manly, anyway.

Now they stretched themselves out on their elbows and
began to puff, charily, and with slender confidence. The
smoke had an unpleasant taste, and they gagged a little, but
Tom said:

"Why it's just as easy! If I'd a knowed *this* was all, I'd a
learnt long ago."

"So would I," said Joe. "It's just nothing."

"Why many a time I've looked at people smoking, and
thought well I wish I could do that; but I never thought I
could," said Tom.

"That's just the way with me, hain't it Huck? You've heard
me talk just that way—haven't you Huck? I'll leave it to Huck
if I haven't."

"Yes—heaps of times," said Huck.

"Well I have too," said Tom; "O, hundreds of times. Once down by the slaughter-house. Don't you remember, Huck? Bob Tanner was there, and Johnny Miller, and Jeff Thatcher, when I said it. Don't you remember Huck, 'bout me saying that?"

"Yes, that's so," said Huck. "That was the day after I lost a white alley. No, 'twas the day before."

"There—I told you so," said Tom. "Huck recollects it."

"I bleeve I could smoke this pipe all day," said Joe. "I don't feel sick."

"Neither do I," said Tom. "*I* could smoke it all day. But I bet you Jeff Thatcher couldn't."

"Jeff Thatcher! Why he'd keel over just with two draws. Just let him try it once. *He'd* see!"

"I bet he would. And Johnny Miller—I wish I could see Johnny Miller tackle it once."

"O, don't *I*!" said Joe. "Why I bet you Johnny Miller couldn't any more do this than nothing. Just one little snifter would fetch *him*."

" 'Deed it would, Joe. Say—I wish the boys could see us now."

"So do I."

"Say—boys, don't say anything about it, and some time when they're around, I'll come up to you and say 'Joe, got a pipe? I want a smoke.' And you'll say, kind of careless like, as if it warn't anything, you'll say, 'Yes, I got my *old* pipe, and another one, but my tobacker ain't very good.' And I'll say,

'Oh, that's all right, if it's *strong* enough.' And then you'll out with the pipes, and we'll light up just as ca'm, and then just see 'em look!"

"By jings that'll be gay, Tom! I wish it was *now*!"

"So do I! And when we tell 'em we learned when we was off pirating, won't they wish they'd been along?"

"O, I reckon not! I'll just *bet* they will!"

So the talk ran on. But presently it began to flag a trifle, and grow disjointed. The silences widened; the expectoration marvelously increased. Every pore inside the boys' cheeks became a spouting fountain; they could scarcely bail out the cellars under their tongues fast enough to prevent an inundation; little overflowings down their throats occurred in spite of all they could do, and sudden retchings followed every time. Both boys were looking very pale and miserable, now. Joe's pipe dropped from his nerveless fingers. Tom's followed. Both fountains were going furiously and both pumps bailing with might and main. Joe said feebly:

"I've lost my knife. I reckon I better go and find it."

Tom said, with quivering lips and halting utterance:

"I'll help you. You go over that way and I'll hunt around by the spring. No, you needn't come, Huck—we can find it."

So Huck sat down again, and waited an hour. Then he found it lonesome, and went to find his comrades. They were wide apart in the woods, both very pale, both fast asleep. But something informed him that if they had had any trouble they had got rid of it.

They were not talkative at supper that night. They had a humble look, and when Huck prepared his pipe after the meal and was going to prepare theirs, they said no, they were not feeling very well—something they ate at dinner had disagreed with them.

(from The Adventures of Tom Sawyer, *1876, chapter 16)*

THE CADET.

Reforming Sinners

*Nothing so needs reforming
as other people's habits.*

A Cigar as Big as a Crutch

Mark Twain learned early in life the futility of trying to reform his bad habits by taking pledges.

I used to take pledges—and soon violate them. My will was not strong, and I could not help it. And then, to be tied in any way naturally irks an otherwise free person and makes him chafe in his bonds and want to get his liberty. But when I finally ceased from taking definite pledges, and merely resolved that I would kill an injurious desire, but leave myself free to resume the desire and the habit whenever I should choose to do so, I had no more trouble. . . .

When I was a youth I used to take all kinds of pledges, and do my best to keep them, but I never could, because I didn't strike at the root of the habit—the *desire*; I generally broke down within the month. Once I tried limiting a habit. That worked tolerably well for a while. I pledged myself to smoke but one cigar a day. I kept the cigar waiting until bedtime, then I had a luxurious time with it. But desire persecuted me every day and all day long; so, within the week I found myself hunting for larger cigars than I had been used to smoke; then larger ones still, and still larger ones. Within the fortnight I was getting cigars *made* for me—on a yet larger pattern. They still grew and grew in size. Within the month my cigar had grown to such proportions that I could have used it as a crutch. It now seemed to me that a one-cigar limit

was no real protection to a person, so I knocked my pledge
on the head and resumed my liberty.

(from Following the Equator, *1897, chapter* 1*)*

A Youthful Reformer

*One of Mark Twain's most sustained efforts at personal
reform during his youth came during his brief membership in
the Cadets of Temperance.*

*I*n Hannibal, when I was about fifteen, I was for a short time
a Cadet of Temperance, an organization which probably covered the whole United States during as much as a year—possibly even longer. It consisted in a pledge to refrain, during
membership, from the use of tobacco; I mean it consisted
partly in that pledge and partly in a red merino sash, but the
red merino sash was the main part. The boys joined in order
to be privileged to wear it—the pledge part of the matter was
of no consequence. It was so small in importance that, con-
trasted with the sash, it was, in effect, non-existent. The organization was weak and impermanent because there were not
enough holidays to support it. We could turn out and march
and show the red sashes on May Day with the Sunday schools,
and on the Fourth of July with the Sunday schools, the inde-
pendent fire company, and the militia company. But you can't

keep a juvenile moral institution alive on two displays of its sash per year. As a private, I could not have held out beyond one procession, but I was Illustrious Grand Worthy Secretary and Royal Inside Sentinel, and had the privilege of inventing the passwords and of wearing a rosette on my sash. Under these conditions, I was enabled to remain steadfast until I had gathered the glory of two displays—May Day and the Fourth of July. Then I resigned straightway, and straightway left the lodge.

I had not smoked for three full months, and no words can adequately describe the smoke appetite that was consuming me. I had been a smoker from my ninth year—a private one during the first two years, but a public one after that—that is to say, after my father's death. I was smoking, and utterly happy, before I was thirty steps from the lodge door. I do not now know what the brand of the cigar was. It was probably not choice, or the previous smoker would not have thrown it away so soon. But I realized that it was the best cigar that was ever made. The previous smoker would have thought the same if he had been without a smoke for three months. I smoked that stub without shame. I could not do it now without shame, because now I am more refined than I was then. But I would smoke it, just the same. I know myself, and I know the human race, well enough to know that.

(from his autobiography)

In The Adventures of Tom Sawyer, *Tom joins the Cadets of
Temperance for much the same reasons that Mark Twain
did—and with much the same results.*

Tom joined the new order of Cadets of Temperance, being
attracted by the showy character of their "regalia." He prom-
ised to abstain from smoking, chewing and profanity as long
as he remained a member. Now he found out a new thing—
namely, that to promise not to do a thing is the surest way in
the world to make a body want to go and do that very thing.
Tom soon found himself tormented with a desire to drink and
swear; the desire grew to be so intense that nothing but the
hope of a chance to display himself in his red sash kept him
from withdrawing from the order. Fourth of July was coming; but he soon gave that up—gave it up before he had worn
his shackles over forty-eight hours—and fixed his hopes upon
old Judge Frazer, justice of the peace, who was apparently on
his death-bed and would have a big public funeral, since he
was so high an official. During three days Tom was deeply
concerned about the Judge's condition and hungry for news
of it. Sometimes his hopes ran high—so high that he would
venture to get out his regalia and practice before the looking
glass. But the Judge had a most discouraging way of fluctu-
ating. At last he was pronounced upon the mend—and then
convalescent. Tom was disgusted; and felt a sense of injury,
too. He handed in his resignation at once—and that night the

Judge suffered a relapse and died. Tom resolved that he would never trust a man like that again.

The funeral was a fine thing. The Cadets paraded in a style calculated to kill the late member with envy. Tom was a free boy again, however—there was something in that. He could drink and swear, now—but found to his surprise that he did not want to. The simple fact that he could, took the desire away, and the charm of it. . . .

(from The Adventures of Tom Sawyer, *1876, chapter 22)*

A Soft Name for Stealing

As Huck and Jim flee down the Mississippi River in Adventures of Huckleberry Finn, *Huck explains how they got around having to "steal" their food.*

*E*very night, now, I used to slip ashore, towards ten o'clock, at some little village, and buy ten or fifteen cents' worth of meal or bacon or other stuff to eat; and sometimes I lifted a chicken that warn't roosting comfortable, and took him along. Pap always said, take a chicken when you get a chance, because if you don't want him yourself you can easy find somebody that does, and a good deed ain't ever forgot. I never see pap when he didn't want the chicken himself, but that is what he used to say, anyway.

Mornings, before daylight, I slipped into cornfields and borrowed a watermelon, or a mush-melon, or a punkin, or some new corn, or things of that kind. Pap always said it warn't no harm to borrow things, if you was meaning to pay them back, sometime; but the widow said it warn't anything but a soft name for stealing, and no decent body would do it. Jim said he reckoned the widow was partly right and pap was partly right; so the best way would be for us to pick out two or three things from the list and say we wouldn't borrow them any more—then he reckoned it wouldn't be no harm to borrow the others. So we talked it over all one night, drifting along down the river, trying to make up our minds whether to drop the watermelons, or the cantelopes, or the mushmelons, or what. But towards daylight we got it all settled satisfactory, and concluded to drop crabapples and p'simmons. We warn't feeling just right, before that, but it was all comfortable now. I was glad the way it come out, too, because crabapples ain't ever good, and the p'simmons wouldn't be ripe for two or three months yet.

(from Adventures of Huckleberry Finn, *1884, chapter 12)*

A Whisper to Parents

*It is a wise child that knows its own father,
and an unusual one that unreservedly approves of him.*

*We think boys are rude, unsensitive animals but it is
not so in all cases. Each boy has one or two sensitive spots
and if you can find out where they are located you have
only to touch them and you can scorch him as with fire.*

Boys Will Be Boys

In A Connecticut Yankee at King Arthur's Court, *Hank Morgan goes on a knightly quest. Dressed in splendid armor and mounted (with help from several men) on a magnificent steed, Hank rides off from Camelot. His rough treatment at the hands of village boys typifies the disrespectful behavior of boys in all times and all places.*

*A*nd so we started; and everybody gave us a goodbye and waved their handkerchiefs or helmets. And everybody we met, going down the hill and through the village was respectful to us, except some shabby little boys on the outskirts. They said—

"Oh, what a guy!" And hove clods at us.

In my experience boys are the same in all ages. They don't respect anything, they don't care for anything or anybody. They say "Go up, baldhead" to the prophet going his unoffending way in the gray of antiquity; they sass me in the holy gloom of the Middle Ages; and I had seen them act the same way in Buchanan's administration; I remember, because I was there and helped. The prophet had his bears and settled with his boys; and I wanted to get down and settle with mine, but it wouldn't answer, because I couldn't have got up again [on his horse]. I hate a country without a derrick.

(from A Connecticut Yankee at King Arthur's Court, *1889, chapter 11)*

Advice to Parents on Curing Their Children

During his stay at San Francisco's Lick House hotel in 1863, Mark Twain was plagued by undisciplined children running wild. His advice on treating unruly children might apply equally well today.

*H*ere come those young savages again—those noisy and inevitable children. God be with them!—or they with him, rather, if it be not asking too much. . . . They have driven me from labor many and many a time; but behold! the hour of retribution is at hand. . . .

It is a living wonder to me that I haven't scalped some of those children before now. I expect that I would have done it, but then I hardly felt well enough acquainted with them. I scarcely ever show them any attention anyhow, unless it is to throw a boot-jack at them or some little nonsense of that kind when I happen to feel playful. I am confident I would have destroyed several of them though, only it might appear as if I were making most too free.

I observe that the young officer of the Pacific Squadron— the one with his nostrils turned up like port-holes—has become a great favorite with half the mothers in the house, by imparting to them much useful information concerning the manner of doctoring children among the South American savages. His brother is brigadier in the Navy. The drabcomplexioned youth with the Solferino mustache has corralled the other half with the Japanese treatment. The more I think of it the more I admire it. Now, I am no peanut. I have an idea that I could invent some little remedies that would stir up a commotion among these women, if I chose to try I always had a good general notion of physic, I believe. It is one of my natural gifts, too, for I have never studied a single day under a regular physician. I will jot down a few items here, just to see how likely I am to succeed.

In the matter of measles, the idea is, to bring it out—bring it to the surface. Take the child and fill it up with saffron tea. Add something to make the patient sleep—say a tablespoonful of arsenic. Don't rock it—it will sleep anyhow.

As far as brain fever is concerned: This is a very dangerous disease, and must be treated with decision and dispatch. In every case where it has proved fatal, the sufferer invariably perished. You must strike at the root of the distemper. Remove the brains; and then—Well, that will be sufficient—that will answer—just remove the brains. This remedy has never been known to fail. It was originated by the lamented J. W. Macbeth, Thane of Cawdor, Scotland, who refers to it thus: "Time was, that when the brains were out, the man would die; but, under different circumstances, I think not; and, all things being equal, I believe you, my boy." Those were his last words.

Concerning worms: Administer a catfish three times a week. Keep the room very quiet; the fish won't bite if there is the least noise.

When you come to fits, take no chances on fits. If the child has them bad, soak it in a barrel of rain-water over night, or a good article of vinegar. If this does not put an end to its troubles, soak it a week. You can't soak a child too much when it has fits.

In cases wherein an infant stammers, remove the under-jaw. In proof of the efficacy of this treatment, I append the following certificate, voluntarily forwarded to me by Mr. Zeb. Leavenworth, of St. Louis, Mo.:

ST. LOUIS, MAY 26, 1863

Mr. Mark Twain—Dear Sir:—Under Providence, I am beholden to you for the salvation of my Johnny. For a matter of three years, that suffering child stuttered to that degree that it was a pain a sorrow to me to hear him stagger over the sacred name of "p-p-p-pap." It troubled me so that I neglected my business; I refused food; I took no pride in my dress, and my hair actually began to fall off. I could not rest; I could not sleep. Morning, noon, and night, I did nothing but moan pitifully, and murmur to myself: "Hell's fire! what am I going to do about my Johnny?" But in a blessed hour you appeared unto me like an angel from the skies; and without hope of reward, revealed your sovereign remedy—and that very day, I sawed off my Johnny's underjaw. May Heaven bless you, noble Sir. It afforded instant relief; and my Johnny has never stammered since. I honestly believe he never will again. As to disfigurement, he does seem to look sorter ornery and hog-mouthed, but I am too grateful in having got him effectually saved from that dreadful stuttering, to make much account of small matters. Heaven speed you in your holy work of healing the afflictions of humanity. And if my poor testimony can be of any service to you, do with it as you think will result in the greatest good to our fellow-creatures. Once more, Heaven bless you.

Zeb. Leavenworth

Now, that has such a plausible ring about it, that I can hardly keep from believing it myself. I consider it a very fair success.

Regarding Cramps. Take your offspring—let the same be warm and dry at the time—and immerse it in a commodious soup-tureen filled with the best quality of camphene. Place it over a slow fire, and add reasonable quantities of pepper, mustard, horse-radish, saltpetre, strychnine, blue vitriol, aqua fortis, a quart of flour, and eight or ten fresh eggs, stirring it from time to time, to keep up a healthy reaction. Let it simmer fifteen minutes. When your child is done, set the tureen off, and allow the infallible remedy to cool. If this does not confer an entire insensibility to cramps, you must lose no time, for the case is desperate. Take your offspring, and parboil it. The most vindictive cramps cannot survive this treatment; neither can the subject, unless it is endowed with an iron constitution. It is an extreme measure, and I always dislike to resort to it. I never parboil a child until everything else has failed to bring about the desired end.

Well, I think those will do to commence with. I can branch out, you know, when I get more confidence in myself. . . .

(from "Those Blasted Children," originally published in New York Saturday Mercury, February 21, 1864)